C-116 CAREER EXAMINATION SERIES

This is your PASSBOOK for...

Public Safety Dispatcher I

Test Preparation Study Guide Questions & Answers

NLC®
NATIONAL LEARNING CORPORATION®

National Learning Corporation

212 Michael Drive, Syosset, NY 11791
(516) 921-8888 • www.passbooks.com
E-mail: info@passbooks.com

PUBLISHED IN THE UNITED STATES OF AMERICA

PASSBOOK® SERIES

THE *PASSBOOK® SERIES* has been created to prepare applicants and candidates for the ultimate academic battlefield – the examination room.

At some time in our lives, each and every one of us may be required to take an examination – for validation, matriculation, admission, qualification, registration, certification, or licensure.

Based on the assumption that every applicant or candidate has met the basic formal educational standards, has taken the required number of courses, and read the necessary texts, the *PASSBOOK® SERIES* furnishes the one special preparation which may assure passing with confidence, instead of failing with insecurity. Examination questions – together with answers – are furnished as the basic vehicle for study so that the mysteries of the examination and its compounding difficulties may be eliminated or diminished by a sure method.

This book is meant to help you pass your examination provided that you qualify and are serious in your objective.

The entire field is reviewed through the huge store of content information which is succinctly presented through a provocative and challenging approach – the question-and-answer method.

A climate of success is established by furnishing the correct answers at the end of each test.

You soon learn to recognize types of questions, forms of questions, and patterns of questioning. You may even begin to anticipate expected outcomes.

You perceive that many questions are repeated or adapted so that you can gain acute insights, which may enable you to score many sure points.

You learn how to confront new questions, or types of questions, and to attack them confidently and work out the correct answers.

You note objectives and emphases, and recognize pitfalls and dangers, so that you may make positive educational adjustments.

Moreover, you are kept fully informed in relation to new concepts, methods, practices, and directions in the field.

You discover that you are actually taking the examination all the time: you are preparing for the examination by "taking" an examination, not by reading extraneous and/or supererogatory textbooks.

In short, this PASSBOOK®, used directedly, should be an important factor in helping you to pass your test.

PUBLIC SAFETY DISPATCHER I

DUTIES

Operates a two-way radio communications system to dispatch public safety personnel to calls for assistance. May operate a telephone switchboard or complaint receiving system which receives requests from the public for police or other public safety assistance. May operate a computer terminal to obtain information on active warrants and to update the computer file. May receive and transmit messages on a nationwide teletype system, joined with Federal, State and local agencies, the Armed Forces and the Attorney General's Office. Performs related work as required.

SCOPE OF THE EXAMINATION

The written test will cover knowledge, skills and/or abilities in such areas as:

1. Understanding and interpreting written material including procedures;
2. Comparing and verifying alpha and numeric characters;
3. Coding and decoding information; and
4. Map reading.

HOW TO TAKE A TEST

I. YOU MUST PASS AN EXAMINATION

A. WHAT EVERY CANDIDATE SHOULD KNOW

Examination applicants often ask us for help in preparing for the written test. What can I study in advance? What kinds of questions will be asked? How will the test be given? How will the papers be graded?

As an applicant for a civil service examination, you may be wondering about some of these things. Our purpose here is to suggest effective methods of advance study and to describe civil service examinations.

Your chances for success on this examination can be increased if you know how to prepare. Those "pre-examination jitters" can be reduced if you know what to expect. You can even experience an adventure in good citizenship if you know why civil service exams are given.

B. WHY ARE CIVIL SERVICE EXAMINATIONS GIVEN?

Civil service examinations are important to you in two ways. As a citizen, you want public jobs filled by employees who know how to do their work. As a job seeker, you want a fair chance to compete for that job on an equal footing with other candidates. The best-known means of accomplishing this two-fold goal is the competitive examination.

Exams are widely publicized throughout the nation. They may be administered for jobs in federal, state, city, municipal, town or village governments or agencies.

Any citizen may apply, with some limitations, such as the age or residence of applicants. Your experience and education may be reviewed to see whether you meet the requirements for the particular examination. When these requirements exist, they are reasonable and applied consistently to all applicants. Thus, a competitive examination may cause you some uneasiness now, but it is your privilege and safeguard.

C. HOW ARE CIVIL SERVICE EXAMS DEVELOPED?

Examinations are carefully written by trained technicians who are specialists in the field known as "psychological measurement," in consultation with recognized authorities in the field of work that the test will cover. These experts recommend the subject matter areas or skills to be tested; only those knowledges or skills important to your success on the job are included. The most reliable books and source materials available are used as references. Together, the experts and technicians judge the difficulty level of the questions.

Test technicians know how to phrase questions so that the problem is clearly stated. Their ethics do not permit "trick" or "catch" questions. Questions may have been tried out on sample groups, or subjected to statistical analysis, to determine their usefulness.

Written tests are often used in combination with performance tests, ratings of training and experience, and oral interviews. All of these measures combine to form the best-known means of finding the right person for the right job.

II. HOW TO PASS THE WRITTEN TEST

A. NATURE OF THE EXAMINATION

To prepare intelligently for civil service examinations, you should know how they differ from school examinations you have taken. In school you were assigned certain definite pages to read or subjects to cover. The examination questions were quite detailed and usually emphasized memory. Civil service exams, on the other hand, try to discover your present ability to perform the duties of a position, plus your potentiality to learn these duties. In other words, a civil service exam attempts to predict how successful you will be. Questions cover such a broad area that they cannot be as minute and detailed as school exam questions.

In the public service similar kinds of work, or positions, are grouped together in one "class." This process is known as *position-classification.* All the positions in a class are paid according to the salary range for that class. One class title covers all of these positions, and they are all tested by the same examination.

B. FOUR BASIC STEPS

1) Study the announcement

How, then, can you know what subjects to study? Our best answer is: "Learn as much as possible about the class of positions for which you've applied." The exam will test the knowledge, skills and abilities needed to do the work.

Your most valuable source of information about the position you want is the official exam announcement. This announcement lists the training and experience qualifications. Check these standards and apply only if you come reasonably close to meeting them.

The brief description of the position in the examination announcement offers some clues to the subjects which will be tested. Think about the job itself. Review the duties in your mind. Can you perform them, or are there some in which you are rusty? Fill in the blank spots in your preparation.

Many jurisdictions preview the written test in the exam announcement by including a section called "Knowledge and Abilities Required," "Scope of the Examination," or some similar heading. Here you will find out specifically what fields will be tested.

2) Review your own background

Once you learn in general what the position is all about, and what you need to know to do the work, ask yourself which subjects you already know fairly well and which need improvement. You may wonder whether to concentrate on improving your strong areas or on building some background in your fields of weakness. When the announcement has specified "some knowledge" or "considerable knowledge," or has used adjectives like "beginning principles of..." or "advanced ... methods," you can get a clue as to the number and difficulty of questions to be asked in any given field. More questions, and hence broader coverage, would be included for those subjects which are more important in the work. Now weigh your strengths and weaknesses against the job requirements and prepare accordingly.

3) Determine the level of the position

Another way to tell how intensively you should prepare is to understand the level of the job for which you are applying. Is it the entering level? In other words, is this the position in which beginners in a field of work are hired? Or is it an intermediate or advanced level? Sometimes this is indicated by such words as "Junior" or "Senior" in the class title. Other jurisdictions use Roman numerals to designate the level – Clerk I, Clerk II, for example. The word "Supervisor" sometimes appears in the title. If the level is not indicated by the title, check the description of duties. Will you be working under very close supervision, or will you have responsibility for independent decisions in this work?

4) Choose appropriate study materials

Now that you know the subjects to be examined and the relative amount of each subject to be covered, you can choose suitable study materials. For beginning level jobs, or even advanced ones, if you have a pronounced weakness in some aspect of your training, read a modern, standard textbook in that field. Be sure it is up to date and has general coverage. Such books are normally available at your library, and the librarian will be glad to help you locate one. For entry-level positions, questions of appropriate difficulty are chosen – neither highly advanced questions, nor those too simple. Such questions require careful thought but not advanced training.

If the position for which you are applying is technical or advanced, you will read more advanced, specialized material. If you are already familiar with the basic principles of your field, elementary textbooks would waste your time. Concentrate on advanced textbooks and technical periodicals. Think through the concepts and review difficult problems in your field.

These are all general sources. You can get more ideas on your own initiative, following these leads. For example, training manuals and publications of the government agency which employs workers in your field can be useful, particularly for technical and professional positions. A letter or visit to the government department involved may result in more specific study suggestions, and certainly will provide you with a more definite idea of the exact nature of the position you are seeking.

III. KINDS OF TESTS

Tests are used for purposes other than measuring knowledge and ability to perform specified duties. For some positions, it is equally important to test ability to make adjustments to new situations or to profit from training. In others, basic mental abilities not dependent on information are essential. Questions which test these things may not appear as pertinent to the duties of the position as those which test for knowledge and information. Yet they are often highly important parts of a fair examination. For very general questions, it is almost impossible to help you direct your study efforts. What we can do is to point out some of the more common of these general abilities needed in public service positions and describe some typical questions.

1) General information

Broad, general information has been found useful for predicting job success in some kinds of work. This is tested in a variety of ways, from vocabulary lists to questions about current events. Basic background in some field of work, such as sociology or economics, may be sampled in a group of questions. Often these are principles which have become familiar to most persons through exposure rather than through formal training. It is difficult to advise you how to study for these questions; being alert to the world around you is our best suggestion.

2) Verbal ability

An example of an ability needed in many positions is verbal or language ability. Verbal ability is, in brief, the ability to use and understand words. Vocabulary and grammar tests are typical measures of this ability. Reading comprehension or paragraph interpretation questions are common in many kinds of civil service tests. You are given a paragraph of written material and asked to find its central meaning.

3) Numerical ability

Number skills can be tested by the familiar arithmetic problem, by checking paired lists of numbers to see which are alike and which are different, or by interpreting charts and graphs. In the latter test, a graph may be printed in the test booklet which you are asked to use as the basis for answering questions.

4) Observation

A popular test for law-enforcement positions is the observation test. A picture is shown to you for several minutes, then taken away. Questions about the picture test your ability to observe both details and larger elements.

5) Following directions

In many positions in the public service, the employee must be able to carry out written instructions dependably and accurately. You may be given a chart with several columns, each column listing a variety of information. The questions require you to carry out directions involving the information given in the chart.

6) Skills and aptitudes

Performance tests effectively measure some manual skills and aptitudes. When the skill is one in which you are trained, such as typing or shorthand, you can practice. These tests are often very much like those given in business school or high school courses. For many of the other skills and aptitudes, however, no short-time preparation can be made. Skills and abilities natural to you or that you have developed throughout your lifetime are being tested.

Many of the general questions just described provide all the data needed to answer the questions and ask you to use your reasoning ability to find the answers. Your best preparation for these tests, as well as for tests of facts and ideas, is to be at your physical and mental best. You, no doubt, have your own methods of getting into an exam-taking mood and keeping "in shape." The next section lists some ideas on this subject.

IV. KINDS OF QUESTIONS

Only rarely is the "essay" question, which you answer in narrative form, used in civil service tests. Civil service tests are usually of the short-answer type. Full instructions for answering these questions will be given to you at the examination. But in case this is your first experience with short-answer questions and separate answer sheets, here is what you need to know:

1) Multiple-choice Questions

Most popular of the short-answer questions is the "multiple choice" or "best answer" question. It can be used, for example, to test for factual knowledge, ability to solve problems or judgment in meeting situations found at work.

A multiple-choice question is normally one of three types—

- It can begin with an incomplete statement followed by several possible endings. You are to find the one ending which *best* completes the statement, although some of the others may not be entirely wrong.
- It can also be a complete statement in the form of a question which is answered by choosing one of the statements listed.

- It can be in the form of a problem – again you select the best answer.

Here is an example of a multiple-choice question with a discussion which should give you some clues as to the method for choosing the right answer:

When an employee has a complaint about his assignment, the action which will *best* help him overcome his difficulty is to
A. discuss his difficulty with his coworkers
B. take the problem to the head of the organization
C. take the problem to the person who gave him the assignment
D. say nothing to anyone about his complaint

In answering this question, you should study each of the choices to find which is best. Consider choice "A" – Certainly an employee may discuss his complaint with fellow employees, but no change or improvement can result, and the complaint remains unresolved. Choice "B" is a poor choice since the head of the organization probably does not know what assignment you have been given, and taking your problem to him is known as "going over the head" of the supervisor. The supervisor, or person who made the assignment, is the person who can clarify it or correct any injustice. Choice "C" is, therefore, correct. To say nothing, as in choice "D," is unwise. Supervisors have and interest in knowing the problems employees are facing, and the employee is seeking a solution to his problem.

2) True/False Questions

The "true/false" or "right/wrong" form of question is sometimes used. Here a complete statement is given. Your job is to decide whether the statement is right or wrong.

SAMPLE: A roaming cell-phone call to a nearby city costs less than a non-roaming call to a distant city.

This statement is wrong, or false, since roaming calls are more expensive.

This is not a complete list of all possible question forms, although most of the others are variations of these common types. You will always get complete directions for answering questions. Be sure you understand *how* to mark your answers – ask questions until you do.

V. RECORDING YOUR ANSWERS

Computer terminals are used more and more today for many different kinds of exams.

For an examination with very few applicants, you may be told to record your answers in the test booklet itself. Separate answer sheets are much more common. If this separate answer sheet is to be scored by machine – and this is often the case – it is highly important that you mark your answers correctly in order to get credit.

An electronic scoring machine is often used in civil service offices because of the speed with which papers can be scored. Machine-scored answer sheets must be marked with a pencil, which will be given to you. This pencil has a high graphite content which responds to the electronic scoring machine. As a matter of fact, stray dots may register as answers, so do not let your pencil rest on the answer sheet while you are pondering the correct answer. Also, if your pencil lead breaks or is otherwise defective, ask for another.

Since the answer sheet will be dropped in a slot in the scoring machine, be careful not to bend the corners or get the paper crumpled.

The answer sheet normally has five vertical columns of numbers, with 30 numbers to a column. These numbers correspond to the question numbers in your test booklet. After each number, going across the page are four or five pairs of dotted lines. These short dotted lines have small letters or numbers above them. The first two pairs may also have a "T" or "F" above the letters. This indicates that the first two pairs only are to be used if the questions are of the true-false type. If the questions are multiple choice, disregard the "T" and "F" and pay attention only to the small letters or numbers.

Answer your questions in the manner of the sample that follows:

32. The largest city in the United States is
    A. Washington, D.C.
    B. New York City
    C. Chicago
    D. Detroit
    E. San Francisco

1) Choose the answer you think is best. (New York City is the largest, so "B" is correct.)
2) Find the row of dotted lines numbered the same as the question you are answering. (Find row number 32)
3) Find the pair of dotted lines corresponding to the answer. (Find the pair of lines under the mark "B.")
4) Make a solid black mark between the dotted lines.

VI. BEFORE THE TEST

Common sense will help you find procedures to follow to get ready for an examination. Too many of us, however, overlook these sensible measures. Indeed, nervousness and fatigue have been found to be the most serious reasons why applicants fail to do their best on civil service tests. Here is a list of reminders:

- Begin your preparation early – Don't wait until the last minute to go scurrying around for books and materials or to find out what the position is all about.
- Prepare continuously – An hour a night for a week is better than an all-night cram session. This has been definitely established. What is more, a night a week for a month will return better dividends than crowding your study into a shorter period of time.
- Locate the place of the exam – You have been sent a notice telling you when and where to report for the examination. If the location is in a different town or otherwise unfamiliar to you, it would be well to inquire the best route and learn something about the building.
- Relax the night before the test – Allow your mind to rest. Do not study at all that night. Plan some mild recreation or diversion; then go to bed early and get a good night's sleep.
- Get up early enough to make a leisurely trip to the place for the test – This way unforeseen events, traffic snarls, unfamiliar buildings, etc. will not upset you.
- Dress comfortably – A written test is not a fashion show. You will be known by number and not by name, so wear something comfortable.

- Leave excess paraphernalia at home – Shopping bags and odd bundles will get in your way. You need bring only the items mentioned in the official notice you received; usually everything you need is provided. Do not bring reference books to the exam. They will only confuse those last minutes and be taken away from you when in the test room.
- Arrive somewhat ahead of time – If because of transportation schedules you must get there very early, bring a newspaper or magazine to take your mind off yourself while waiting.
- Locate the examination room – When you have found the proper room, you will be directed to the seat or part of the room where you will sit. Sometimes you are given a sheet of instructions to read while you are waiting. Do not fill out any forms until you are told to do so; just read them and be prepared.
- Relax and prepare to listen to the instructions
- If you have any physical problem that may keep you from doing your best, be sure to tell the test administrator. If you are sick or in poor health, you really cannot do your best on the exam. You can come back and take the test some other time.

VII. AT THE TEST

The day of the test is here and you have the test booklet in your hand. The temptation to get going is very strong. Caution! There is more to success than knowing the right answers. You must know how to identify your papers and understand variations in the type of short-answer question used in this particular examination. Follow these suggestions for maximum results from your efforts:

1) Cooperate with the monitor

The test administrator has a duty to create a situation in which you can be as much at ease as possible. He will give instructions, tell you when to begin, check to see that you are marking your answer sheet correctly, and so on. He is not there to guard you, although he will see that your competitors do not take unfair advantage. He wants to help you do your best.

2) Listen to all instructions

Don't jump the gun! Wait until you understand all directions. In most civil service tests you get more time than you need to answer the questions. So don't be in a hurry. Read each word of instructions until you clearly understand the meaning. Study the examples, listen to all announcements and follow directions. Ask questions if you do not understand what to do.

3) Identify your papers

Civil service exams are usually identified by number only. You will be assigned a number; you must not put your name on your test papers. Be sure to copy your number correctly. Since more than one exam may be given, copy your exact examination title.

4) Plan your time

Unless you are told that a test is a "speed" or "rate of work" test, speed itself is usually not important. Time enough to answer all the questions will be provided, but this does not mean that you have all day. An overall time limit has been set. Divide the total time (in minutes) by the number of questions to determine the approximate time you have for each question.

5) Do not linger over difficult questions

If you come across a difficult question, mark it with a paper clip (useful to have along) and come back to it when you have been through the booklet. One caution if you do this – be sure to skip a number on your answer sheet as well. Check often to be sure that you have not lost your place and that you are marking in the row numbered the same as the question you are answering.

6) Read the questions

Be sure you know what the question asks! Many capable people are unsuccessful because they failed to *read* the questions correctly.

7) Answer all questions

Unless you have been instructed that a penalty will be deducted for incorrect answers, it is better to guess than to omit a question.

8) Speed tests

It is often better NOT to guess on speed tests. It has been found that on timed tests people are tempted to spend the last few seconds before time is called in marking answers at random – without even reading them – in the hope of picking up a few extra points. To discourage this practice, the instructions may warn you that your score will be "corrected" for guessing. That is, a penalty will be applied. The incorrect answers will be deducted from the correct ones, or some other penalty formula will be used.

9) Review your answers

If you finish before time is called, go back to the questions you guessed or omitted to give them further thought. Review other answers if you have time.

10) Return your test materials

If you are ready to leave before others have finished or time is called, take ALL your materials to the monitor and leave quietly. Never take any test material with you. The monitor can discover whose papers are not complete, and taking a test booklet may be grounds for disqualification.

VIII. EXAMINATION TECHNIQUES

1) Read the general instructions carefully. These are usually printed on the first page of the exam booklet. As a rule, these instructions refer to the timing of the examination; the fact that you should not start work until the signal and must stop work at a signal, etc. If there are any *special* instructions, such as a choice of questions to be answered, make sure that you note this instruction carefully.

2) When you are ready to start work on the examination, that is as soon as the signal has been given, read the instructions to each question booklet, underline any key words or phrases, such as *least, best, outline, describe* and the like. In this way you will tend to answer as requested rather than discover on reviewing your paper that you *listed without describing*, that you selected the *worst* choice rather than the *best* choice, etc.

3) If the examination is of the objective or multiple-choice type – that is, each question will also give a series of possible answers: A, B, C or D, and you are called upon to select the best answer and write the letter next to that answer on your answer paper – it is advisable to start answering each question in turn. There may be anywhere from 50 to 100 such questions in the three or four hours allotted and you can see how much time would be taken if you read through all the questions before beginning to answer any. Furthermore, if you come across a question or group of questions which you know would be difficult to answer, it would undoubtedly affect your handling of all the other questions.

4) If the examination is of the essay type and contains but a few questions, it is a moot point as to whether you should read all the questions before starting to answer any one. Of course, if you are given a choice – say five out of seven and the like – then it is essential to read all the questions so you can eliminate the two that are most difficult. If, however, you are asked to answer all the questions, there may be danger in trying to answer the easiest one first because you may find that you will spend too much time on it. The best technique is to answer the first question, then proceed to the second, etc.

5) Time your answers. Before the exam begins, write down the time it started, then add the time allowed for the examination and write down the time it must be completed, then divide the time available somewhat as follows:
   - If 3-1/2 hours are allowed, that would be 210 minutes. If you have 80 objective-type questions, that would be an average of 2-1/2 minutes per question. Allow yourself no more than 2 minutes per question, or a total of 160 minutes, which will permit about 50 minutes to review.
   - If for the time allotment of 210 minutes there are 7 essay questions to answer, that would average about 30 minutes a question. Give yourself only 25 minutes per question so that you have about 35 minutes to review.

6) The most important instruction is to *read each question* and make sure you know what is wanted. The second most important instruction is to *time yourself properly* so that you answer every question. The third most important instruction is to *answer every question*. Guess if you have to but include something for each question. Remember that you will receive no credit for a blank and will probably receive some credit if you write something in answer to an essay question. If you guess a letter – say "B" for a multiple-choice question – you may have guessed right. If you leave a blank as an answer to a multiple-choice question, the examiners may respect your feelings but it will not add a point to your score. Some exams may penalize you for wrong answers, so in such cases *only*, you may not want to guess unless you have some basis for your answer.

7) Suggestions
   a. Objective-type questions
      1. Examine the question booklet for proper sequence of pages and questions
      2. Read all instructions carefully
      3. Skip any question which seems too difficult; return to it after all other questions have been answered
      4. Apportion your time properly; do not spend too much time on any single question or group of questions

5. Note and underline key words – *all, most, fewest, least, best, worst, same, opposite,* etc.
6. Pay particular attention to negatives
7. Note unusual option, e.g., unduly long, short, complex, different or similar in content to the body of the question
8. Observe the use of "hedging" words – *probably, may, most likely,* etc.
9. Make sure that your answer is put next to the same number as the question
10. Do not second-guess unless you have good reason to believe the second answer is definitely more correct
11. Cross out original answer if you decide another answer is more accurate; do not erase until you are ready to hand your paper in
12. Answer all questions; guess unless instructed otherwise
13. Leave time for review

b. Essay questions

1. Read each question carefully
2. Determine exactly what is wanted. Underline key words or phrases.
3. Decide on outline or paragraph answer
4. Include many different points and elements unless asked to develop any one or two points or elements
5. Show impartiality by giving pros and cons unless directed to select one side only
6. Make and write down any assumptions you find necessary to answer the questions
7. Watch your English, grammar, punctuation and choice of words
8. Time your answers; don't crowd material

8) Answering the essay question

Most essay questions can be answered by framing the specific response around several key words or ideas. Here are a few such key words or ideas:

M's: manpower, materials, methods, money, management
P's: purpose, program, policy, plan, procedure, practice, problems, pitfalls, personnel, public relations

a. Six basic steps in handling problems:

1. Preliminary plan and background development
2. Collect information, data and facts
3. Analyze and interpret information, data and facts
4. Analyze and develop solutions as well as make recommendations
5. Prepare report and sell recommendations
6. Install recommendations and follow up effectiveness

b. Pitfalls to avoid

1. *Taking things for granted* – A statement of the situation does not necessarily imply that each of the elements is necessarily true; for example, a complaint may be invalid and biased so that all that can be taken for granted is that a complaint has been registered

2. *Considering only one side of a situation* – Wherever possible, indicate several alternatives and then point out the reasons you selected the best one
3. *Failing to indicate follow up* – Whenever your answer indicates action on your part, make certain that you will take proper follow-up action to see how successful your recommendations, procedures or actions turn out to be
4. *Taking too long in answering any single question* – Remember to time your answers properly

IX. AFTER THE TEST

Scoring procedures differ in detail among civil service jurisdictions although the general principles are the same. Whether the papers are hand-scored or graded by machine we have described, they are nearly always graded by number. That is, the person who marks the paper knows only the number – never the name – of the applicant. Not until all the papers have been graded will they be matched with names. If other tests, such as training and experience or oral interview ratings have been given, scores will be combined. Different parts of the examination usually have different weights. For example, the written test might count 60 percent of the final grade, and a rating of training and experience 40 percent. In many jurisdictions, veterans will have a certain number of points added to their grades.

After the final grade has been determined, the names are placed in grade order and an eligible list is established. There are various methods for resolving ties between those who get the same final grade – probably the most common is to place first the name of the person whose application was received first. Job offers are made from the eligible list in the order the names appear on it. You will be notified of your grade and your rank as soon as all these computations have been made. This will be done as rapidly as possible.

People who are found to meet the requirements in the announcement are called "eligibles." Their names are put on a list of eligible candidates. An eligible's chances of getting a job depend on how high he stands on this list and how fast agencies are filling jobs from the list.

When a job is to be filled from a list of eligibles, the agency asks for the names of people on the list of eligibles for that job. When the civil service commission receives this request, it sends to the agency the names of the three people highest on this list. Or, if the job to be filled has specialized requirements, the office sends the agency the names of the top three persons who meet these requirements from the general list.

The appointing officer makes a choice from among the three people whose names were sent to him. If the selected person accepts the appointment, the names of the others are put back on the list to be considered for future openings.

That is the rule in hiring from all kinds of eligible lists, whether they are for typist, carpenter, chemist, or something else. For every vacancy, the appointing officer has his choice of any one of the top three eligibles on the list. This explains why the person whose name is on top of the list sometimes does not get an appointment when some of the persons lower on the list do. If the appointing officer chooses the second or third eligible, the No. 1 eligible does not get a job at once, but stays on the list until he is appointed or the list is terminated.

X. HOW TO PASS THE INTERVIEW TEST

The examination for which you applied requires an oral interview test. You have already taken the written test and you are now being called for the interview test – the final part of the formal examination.

You may think that it is not possible to prepare for an interview test and that there are no procedures to follow during an interview. Our purpose is to point out some things you can do in advance that will help you and some good rules to follow and pitfalls to avoid while you are being interviewed.

What is an interview supposed to test?

The written examination is designed to test the technical knowledge and competence of the candidate; the oral is designed to evaluate intangible qualities, not readily measured otherwise, and to establish a list showing the relative fitness of each candidate – as measured against his competitors – for the position sought. Scoring is not on the basis of "right" and "wrong," but on a sliding scale of values ranging from "not passable" to "outstanding." As a matter of fact, it is possible to achieve a relatively low score without a single "incorrect" answer because of evident weakness in the qualities being measured.

Occasionally, an examination may consist entirely of an oral test – either an individual or a group oral. In such cases, information is sought concerning the technical knowledges and abilities of the candidate, since there has been no written examination for this purpose. More commonly, however, an oral test is used to supplement a written examination.

Who conducts interviews?

The composition of oral boards varies among different jurisdictions. In nearly all, a representative of the personnel department serves as chairman. One of the members of the board may be a representative of the department in which the candidate would work. In some cases, "outside experts" are used, and, frequently, a businessman or some other representative of the general public is asked to serve. Labor and management or other special groups may be represented. The aim is to secure the services of experts in the appropriate field.

However the board is composed, it is a good idea (and not at all improper or unethical) to ascertain in advance of the interview who the members are and what groups they represent. When you are introduced to them, you will have some idea of their backgrounds and interests, and at least you will not stutter and stammer over their names.

What should be done before the interview?

While knowledge about the board members is useful and takes some of the surprise element out of the interview, there is other preparation which is more substantive. It *is* possible to prepare for an oral interview – in several ways:

1) Keep a copy of your application and review it carefully before the interview

This may be the only document before the oral board, and the starting point of the interview. Know what education and experience you have listed there, and the sequence and dates of all of it. Sometimes the board will ask you to review the highlights of your experience for them; you should not have to hem and haw doing it.

2) Study the class specification and the examination announcement

Usually, the oral board has one or both of these to guide them. The qualities, characteristics or knowledges required by the position sought are stated in these documents. They offer valuable clues as to the nature of the oral interview. For example, if the job involves supervisory responsibilities, the announcement will usually indicate that knowledge of modern supervisory methods and the qualifications of the candidate as a supervisor will be tested. If so, you can expect such questions, frequently in the form of a hypothetical situation which you are expected to solve. NEVER go into an oral without knowledge of the duties and responsibilities of the job you seek.

3) Think through each qualification required

Try to visualize the kind of questions you would ask if you were a board member. How well could you answer them? Try especially to appraise your own knowledge and background in each area, *measured against the job sought*, and identify any areas in which you are weak. Be critical and realistic – do not flatter yourself.

4) Do some general reading in areas in which you feel you may be weak

For example, if the job involves supervision and your past experience has NOT, some general reading in supervisory methods and practices, particularly in the field of human relations, might be useful. Do NOT study agency procedures or detailed manuals. The oral board will be testing your understanding and capacity, not your memory.

5) Get a good night's sleep and watch your general health and mental attitude

You will want a clear head at the interview. Take care of a cold or any other minor ailment, and of course, no hangovers.

What should be done on the day of the interview?

Now comes the day of the interview itself. Give yourself plenty of time to get there. Plan to arrive somewhat ahead of the scheduled time, particularly if your appointment is in the fore part of the day. If a previous candidate fails to appear, the board might be ready for you a bit early. By early afternoon an oral board is almost invariably behind schedule if there are many candidates, and you may have to wait. Take along a book or magazine to read, or your application to review, but leave any extraneous material in the waiting room when you go in for your interview. In any event, relax and compose yourself.

The matter of dress is important. The board is forming impressions about you – from your experience, your manners, your attitude, and your appearance. Give your personal appearance careful attention. Dress your best, but not your flashiest. Choose conservative, appropriate clothing, and be sure it is immaculate. This is a business interview, and your appearance should indicate that you regard it as such. Besides, being well groomed and properly dressed will help boost your confidence.

Sooner or later, someone will call your name and escort you into the interview room. *This is it.* From here on you are on your own. It is too late for any more preparation. But remember, you asked for this opportunity to prove your fitness, and you are here because your request was granted.

What happens when you go in?

The usual sequence of events will be as follows: The clerk (who is often the board stenographer) will introduce you to the chairman of the oral board, who will introduce you to the other members of the board. Acknowledge the introductions before you sit down. Do not be surprised if you find a microphone facing you or a stenotypist sitting by. Oral interviews are usually recorded in the event of an appeal or other review.

Usually the chairman of the board will open the interview by reviewing the highlights of your education and work experience from your application – primarily for the benefit of the other members of the board, as well as to get the material into the record. Do not interrupt or comment unless there is an error or significant misinterpretation; if that is the case, do not hesitate. But do not quibble about insignificant matters. Also, he will usually ask you some question about your education, experience or your present job – partly to get you to start talking and to establish the interviewing "rapport." He may start the actual questioning, or turn it over to one of the other members. Frequently, each member undertakes the questioning on a particular area, one in which he is perhaps most competent, so you can expect each member to participate in the examination. Because time is limited, you may also expect some rather abrupt switches in the direction the questioning takes, so do not be upset by it. Normally, a board member will not pursue a single line of questioning unless he discovers a particular strength or weakness.

After each member has participated, the chairman will usually ask whether any member has any further questions, then will ask you if you have anything you wish to add. Unless you are expecting this question, it may floor you. Worse, it may start you off on an extended, extemporaneous speech. The board is not usually seeking more information. The question is principally to offer you a last opportunity to present further qualifications or to indicate that you have nothing to add. So, if you feel that a significant qualification or characteristic has been overlooked, it is proper to point it out in a sentence or so. Do not compliment the board on the thoroughness of their examination – they have been sketchy, and you know it. If you wish, merely say, "No thank you, I have nothing further to add." This is a point where you can "talk yourself out" of a good impression or fail to present an important bit of information. Remember, *you close the interview yourself.*

The chairman will then say, "That is all, Mr. _______, thank you." Do not be startled; the interview is over, and quicker than you think. Thank him, gather your belongings and take your leave. Save your sigh of relief for the other side of the door.

How to put your best foot forward

Throughout this entire process, you may feel that the board individually and collectively is trying to pierce your defenses, seek out your hidden weaknesses and embarrass and confuse you. Actually, this is not true. They are obliged to make an appraisal of your qualifications for the job you are seeking, and they want to see you in your best light. Remember, they must interview all candidates and a non-cooperative candidate may become a failure in spite of their best efforts to bring out his qualifications. Here are 15 suggestions that will help you:

1) Be natural – Keep your attitude confident, not cocky

If you are not confident that you can do the job, do not expect the board to be. Do not apologize for your weaknesses, try to bring out your strong points. The board is interested in a positive, not negative, presentation. Cockiness will antagonize any board member and make him wonder if you are covering up a weakness by a false show of strength.

2) Get comfortable, but don't lounge or sprawl

Sit erectly but not stiffly. A careless posture may lead the board to conclude that you are careless in other things, or at least that you are not impressed by the importance of the occasion. Either conclusion is natural, even if incorrect. Do not fuss with your clothing, a pencil or an ashtray. Your hands may occasionally be useful to emphasize a point; do not let them become a point of distraction.

3) Do not wisecrack or make small talk

This is a serious situation, and your attitude should show that you consider it as such. Further, the time of the board is limited – they do not want to waste it, and neither should you.

4) Do not exaggerate your experience or abilities

In the first place, from information in the application or other interviews and sources, the board may know more about you than you think. Secondly, you probably will not get away with it. An experienced board is rather adept at spotting such a situation, so do not take the chance.

5) If you know a board member, do not make a point of it, yet do not hide it

Certainly you are not fooling him, and probably not the other members of the board. Do not try to take advantage of your acquaintanceship – it will probably do you little good.

6) Do not dominate the interview

Let the board do that. They will give you the clues – do not assume that you have to do all the talking. Realize that the board has a number of questions to ask you, and do not try to take up all the interview time by showing off your extensive knowledge of the answer to the first one.

7) Be attentive

You only have 20 minutes or so, and you should keep your attention at its sharpest throughout. When a member is addressing a problem or question to you, give him your undivided attention. Address your reply principally to him, but do not exclude the other board members.

8) Do not interrupt

A board member may be stating a problem for you to analyze. He will ask you a question when the time comes. Let him state the problem, and wait for the question.

9) Make sure you understand the question

Do not try to answer until you are sure what the question is. If it is not clear, restate it in your own words or ask the board member to clarify it for you. However, do not haggle about minor elements.

10) Reply promptly but not hastily

A common entry on oral board rating sheets is "candidate responded readily," or "candidate hesitated in replies." Respond as promptly and quickly as you can, but do not jump to a hasty, ill-considered answer.

11) Do not be peremptory in your answers

A brief answer is proper – but do not fire your answer back. That is a losing game from your point of view. The board member can probably ask questions much faster than you can answer them.

12) Do not try to create the answer you think the board member wants

He is interested in what kind of mind you have and how it works – not in playing games. Furthermore, he can usually spot this practice and will actually grade you down on it.

13) Do not switch sides in your reply merely to agree with a board member

Frequently, a member will take a contrary position merely to draw you out and to see if you are willing and able to defend your point of view. Do not start a debate, yet do not surrender a good position. If a position is worth taking, it is worth defending.

14) Do not be afraid to admit an error in judgment if you are shown to be wrong

The board knows that you are forced to reply without any opportunity for careful consideration. Your answer may be demonstrably wrong. If so, admit it and get on with the interview.

15) Do not dwell at length on your present job

The opening question may relate to your present assignment. Answer the question but do not go into an extended discussion. You are being examined for a *new* job, not your present one. As a matter of fact, try to phrase ALL your answers in terms of the job for which you are being examined.

Basis of Rating

Probably you will forget most of these "do's" and "don'ts" when you walk into the oral interview room. Even remembering them all will not ensure you a passing grade. Perhaps you did not have the qualifications in the first place. But remembering them will help you to put your best foot forward, without treading on the toes of the board members.

Rumor and popular opinion to the contrary notwithstanding, an oral board wants you to make the best appearance possible. They know you are under pressure – but they also want to see how you respond to it as a guide to what your reaction would be under the pressures of the job you seek. They will be influenced by the degree of poise you display, the personal traits you show and the manner in which you respond.

ABOUT THIS BOOK

This book contains tests divided into Examination Sections. Go through each test, answering every question in the margin. We have also attached a sample answer sheet at the back of the book that can be removed and used. At the end of each test look at the answer key and check your answers. On the ones you got wrong, look at the right answer choice and learn. Do not fill in the answers first. Do not memorize the questions and answers, but understand the answer and principles involved. On your test, the questions will likely be different from the samples. Questions are changed and new ones added. If you understand these past questions you should have success with any changes that arise. Tests may consist of several types of questions. We have additional books on each subject should more study be advisable or necessary for you. Finally, the more you study, the better prepared you will be. This book is intended to be the last thing you study before you walk into the examination room. Prior study of relevant texts is also recommended. NLC publishes some of these in our Fundamental Series. Knowledge and good sense are important factors in passing your exam. Good luck also helps. So now study this Passbook, absorb the material contained within and take that knowledge into the examination. Then do your best to pass that exam.

EXAMINATION SECTION

EXAMINATION SECTION
TEST 1

DIRECTIONS: Each question or incomplete statement is followed by several suggested answers or completions. Select the one that BEST answers the question or completes the statement. *PRINT THE LETTER OF THE CORRECT ANSWER IN THE SPACE AT THE RIGHT.*

1. The term for the place at which the control operator function is performed is the 1.____

   A. operating desk
   B. control point
   C. station
   D. manual control location

2. Before transmitting on any frequency, an operator should 2.____

   A. listen to make sure your signal will be heard
   B. make sure the standing-wave ratio on the antenna feed line is high enough
   C. listen to make sure others are not using the frequency
   D. check the antenna for resonance at the selected frequency

3. The _______ sideband is COMMONLY used for 10-meter phone operation. 3.____

   A. lower
   B. upper
   C. amplitude-compandored
   D. double

4. Which type of system does NOT permit the transmission and reception of any signals to take place at the same time? 4.____

   A. Repeater
   B. Simplex
   C. Remote
   D. Duplex

5. Radio emissions are considered *wideband* if their deviation amounts are greater than a MINIMUM of _______ kHz. 5.____

   A. 10
   B. 1
   C. 15
   D. 5

6. When a signal report is referred to as *three three,* 6.____

   A. its contact is serial number thirty-three
   B. it is unreadable and very weak
   C. it is readable with considerable difficulty
   D. its station is located at thirty-three degrees latitude

7. Generally, the type of communications that are capable of the GREATEST range are _______ band. 7.____

   A. low
   B. high
   C. aviation
   D. side

8. For two-way systems situated in and around an urban area, what block of frequencies are allocated for use by mobile telephone services operated by common carriers? _______ MHz. 8.____

   A. 30
   B. 40
   C. 470-512
   D. 900

9. The basic unit of electrical power is the 9.____

   A. ohm
   B. ampere
   C. volt
   D. watt

10. In the radio transmission of speech, the amplification used at the receiver to maintain the natural balance of high and low speech frequencies is referred to as 10.____

A. preemphasis
B. deemphasis
C. loading
D. squelch

11. An antenna that is mounted horizontally would be MOST suitable for the reception of ______ polarized ______. 11.____

A. horizontally; voltages
B. vertically; waves
C. vertically; voltages
D. horizontally; waves

12. What is the PROPER distress call to use when operating a radiotelephone? 12.____

A. MAYDAY B. HELP C. EMERGENCY D. SOS

13. A two-way FM transmitter should be adjusted for a deviation that will produce a bandwidth ______ AM transmitter. 13.____

A. less than that produced by an equivalently modulated
B. greater than that produced by an equivalently modulated
C. equal to that produced by an equivalently modulated
D. that will not be capable of interacting with an

14. The term for the transmission of signals OUTSIDE the intended band is 14.____

A. spurious emissions
B. off-frequency emissions
C. side tones
D. chirping

15. Which of the following is TRUE of FM radio systems? 15.____

A. The frequency is constant and the amplitude is varied.
B. The amplitude is constant and the frequency is varied.
C. The frequency and the amplitude are varied.
D. Neither the frequency nor the amplitude is modulated.

16. During daytime hours, the BEST band for communications over a distance of 200 miles is the ______-m band. 16.____

A. 160 B. 80 C. 40 D. 6

17. A transmission that disturbs other communications is called 17.____

A. transponder signals
B. unidentified transmissions
C. harmful interference
D. interrupted CW

18. A buzzing or hum in the signal of a high-frequency transmitter is USUALLY caused by 18.____

A. an antenna of the wrong length
B. a bad filter capacitor in the power supply
C. energy from another transmitter
D. a badly-designed power output circuit

19. If an operator's signal is extremely strong and perfectly readable, what adjustment should be made to the transmitter? 19.____

A. Turn on the speech processor
B. Turn down the power output
C. Reduce the frequency
D. Reduce the standing-wave ratio

20. What is generally considered to be the reliable range for UHF communications? _______ km. 20.____

A. 20 B. 40 C. 60 D. 80

21. If a transmitter is operated WITHOUT the cover in place, it may 21.____

A. transmit a weak signal
B. transmit a chirping signal
C. transmit onto unintended bands
D. interfere with other transmitters operating on the same frequency

22. In transmitters used to convey speech, the deviation for the given amplitude 22.____

A. increases as the modulation signal increases
B. decreases as the modulation signal increases
C. remains roughly half of the modulation signal
D. is the same regardless of the frequency of the modulation signal

23. The purpose of a limiter in an FM receiver is to limit the 23.____

A. audio output
B. amplitude of the intermediate frequency signal fed to the detector
C. gain of the radio frequency amplifier
D. amplitude of the detected output signal

24. The FASTEST code speed a repeater may use for automatic identification is _______ words per minute. 24.____

A. 10
B. 20
C. 40
D. no limit

25. The purpose of a squelch control is to 25.____

A. set the sensitivity of the squelch circuit
B. squelch all undesired noise signals
C. set the limit of the noise amplitude
D. squelch interference signals

KEY (CORRECT ANSWERS)

1.	B	11.	D
2.	C	12.	A
3.	B	13.	C
4.	B	14.	A
5.	D	15.	B
6.	C	16.	C
7.	A	17.	C
8.	B	18.	B
9.	D	19.	B
10.	B	20.	B

21. C
22. D
23. B
24. B
25. A

TEST 2

DIRECTIONS: Each question or incomplete statement is followed by several suggested answers or completions. Select the one that BEST answers the question or completes the statement. *PRINT THE LETTER OF THE CORRECT ANSWER IN THE SPACE AT THE RIGHT.*

1. The basic unit of electrical resistance is the 1.____

   A. watt B. ampere C. volt D. ohm

2. An autopatch is a device that 2.____

   A. automatically selects the strongest signal to be repeated
   B. allows repeater users to make telephone calls from their stations
   C. locks other repeaters out of important, confidential communications
   D. connects a mobile station to the next repeater if it moves out of range

3. Which of the following is NOT an advantage gained by using a crystal in radio equipment? 3.____
   Increased

   A. power generation B. frequency stability
   C. overtone generation D. frequency accuracy

4. The purpose of a key-operated on/off switch in the main power line of a station is to 4.____

   A. keep the power company from shutting down power during an emergency
   B. protect against failure of the main fuses
   C. turn off the station in the event of an emergency
   D. keep unauthorized persons from using the station

5. For two-way systems situated in and around an urban area, what block of frequencies are allocated for use by citizen two-way users? 5.____
   _______ MHz.

   A. 30 B. 40 C. 470-512 D. 900

6. A reactance tube is used to develop a(n) _______ signal. 6.____

   A. drift-free AM B. FM
   C. SSB D. TTY

7. Messages concerning a person's well-being that are sent into or out of a disaster area are _______ traffic messages. 7.____

   A. routine B. tactical
   C. formal message D. health and welfare

8. A(n) _______ is used to measure standing wave ratio. 8.____

   A. SWR meter B. current bridge
   C. ammeter D. ohmmeter

9. What is the USUAL remedy for an FM hand-held transceiver that is over-deviating? 9.___

A. Talk more loudly into the microphone
B. Change to a higher power level
C. Talk farther from the microphone
D. Allow the transceiver to cool

10. *Backwave radiation* is radiation 10.___

A. from the rear of the antenna
B. leaking from a CW antenna
C. from a CW transmitter with the key open
D. from a phone transmitter during silent periods

11. The input impedance of a grounded-grid amplifer is 11.___

A. low B. moderate C. high D. very high

12. If a dial which reads 4.525 MHz were marked in kilohertz, it would read _______ kHz. 12.___

A. 4,525,000 B. 4525 C. .004525 D. 45.25

13. A ______ system uses a total of three transmission frequencies. 13.___

A. simplex B. duplex C. repeater D. remote

14. The basic unit of frequency is the 14.___

A. hertz
B. ohm
C. ampere
D. wave ratio

15. What type of feedback is required for an oscillator? 15.___

A. Split-phase
B. In-phase
C. Grid-leak
D. Degenerative

16. Cross-band operation of a repeater station is 16.___

A. permitted, but requires a special state license
B. permitted under the regular repeater station license
C. permitted if the repeater receives signals in both bands
D. not permitted under any circumstances

17. If an unlicensed third party is allowed to use your station, what must you do at your center of operations? 17.___

A. Monitor and supervise the third party's participation when communication occurs at below 30 MHz.
B. Continuously monitor and supervise the third party's participation.
C. Key the transmitter and make the station identification.
D. Report the third party to the FCC.

18. Receiver overload is caused by 18.____

A. too much voltage from the power supply
B. interference from a poorly-adjusted volume control
C. too much current from the power supply
D. interference from the signals of a nearby transmitter

19. Equal but opposite signals are required for operating a ______ amplifier. 19.____

A. parallel B. push-pull C. class C D. series

20. The MAIN purpose of shielding a transmitter is to 20.____

A. prevent unwanted radio-frequency radiation
B. keep electronic parts warmer and more stable
C. give low-pass air filter a solid support
D. help the sound quality

21. In an FM signal, whether modulated or unmodulated, the 21.____

A. carrier frequency amplitude is fixed
B. modulating frequency varies
C. carrier frequency varies
D. modulating frequency is fixed

22. For voice operation, the microphone is connected to the 22.____

A. antenna switch B. transceiver
C. power supply D. antenna

23. Harmonic radiation is unwanted signals 23.____

A. that are combined with a 60-Hz hum
B. caused by vibrations from a nearby transmitter
C. at frequencies which are multiples of an operator's chosen frequency
D. which cause skip propagation

24. The LOWEST frequency of electrical energy that is usually known as radio frequency is ______ Hz. 24.____

A. 20 B. 2,000 C. 20,000 D. 200,000

25. What is the term for the kind of interference created by a continuous broad band of numerous unrelated radio frequency pulses? 25.____

A. Chirp B. Oscillation
C. Impulse noise D. Fluctuation noise

KEY (CORRECT ANSWERS)

1.	D	11.	A
2.	B	12.	B
3.	A	13.	B
4.	D	14.	A
5.	C	15.	B
6.	B	16.	D
7.	D	17.	B
8.	A	18.	D
9.	C	19.	B
10.	C	20.	A

21. C
22. B
23. C
24. C
25. D

EXAMINATION SECTION
TEST 1

DIRECTIONS: Each question or incomplete statement is followed by several suggested answers or completions. Select the one that BEST answers the question or completes the statement. *PRINT THE LETTER OF THE CORRECT ANSWER IN THE SPACE AT THE RIGHT.*

Questions 1-3.

DIRECTIONS: Questions 1 through 3 are to be answered SOLELY on the basis of the following passage.

On May 15 at 10:15 A.M., Mr. Price was returning to his home at 220 Kings Walk when he discovered two of his neighbor's apartment doors slightly opened. One neighbor, Mrs. Kagan, who lives alone in Apartment 1C, was away on vacation. The other apartment, IB, is occupied by Martin and Ruth Stone, an elderly couple, who usually take a walk everyday at 10:00 A.M. Fearing a robbery might be taking place, Mr. Price runs downstairs to Mr. White in Apartment BI to call the police. Police Communications Technician Johnson received the call at 10:20 A.M. Mr. Price gave his address and stated that two apartments were possibly being burglarized. Communications Technician Johnson verified the address in the computer and then asked Mr. Price for descriptions of the suspects. He explained that he had not seen anyone, but he believed that they were still inside the building. Communications Technician Johnson immediately notified the dispatcher who assigned two patrol cars at 10:25 A.M., while Mr. Price was still on the phone. Communications Technician Johnson told Mr. Price that the police were responding to the location.

1. Who called Communications Technician Johnson? 1.____

   A. Mrs. Kagan
   B. Mr. White
   C. Mrs. Stone
   D. Mr. Price

2. What time did Communications Technician Johnson receive the call? 2.____
   ______ A.M.

   A. 10:00 B. 10:15 C. 10:20 D. 10:25

3. Which tenant was away on vacation? 3.____
   The tenant in Apartment

   A. 1C B. IB C. BI D. ID

4. Dispatcher Watkins receives the following information regarding a complaint. 4.____
   Place of occurrence: St. James Park
   Complaint: Large group of intoxicated males throwing beer bottles and playing loud music
   Complainant: Oscar Aker
   Complainant's Address: 13 St. James Square, Apt. 2B
   Dispatcher Watkins is not certain if this incident should be reported to 911 or Mr. Aker's local precinct. Dispatcher Watkins is about to notify his supervisor of the call. Which one of the following expresses the above information MOST clearly and accurately?

A. Mr. Aker, who lives at 13 St. James Square, Apt. 2B, called to make a complaint of a large group of intoxicated males who are throwing beer bottles and playing loud music in St. James Park.
B. Mr. Aker, who lives at 13 St. James Square, called to complain about a large group of intoxicated males, in Apt. 2B. They are throwing beer bottles and playing loud music in St. James Park.
C. Mr. Aker of 13 St. James Square, Apt. 2B, called to complain about loud music. There were a large group of intoxicated males throwing beer bottles in St. James Park.
D. As a result of intoxicated males throwing beer bottles Mr. Aker of 13 St. James Square, Apt. 2B, called to complain. A large group was playing loud music in St. James Park.

5. Communications Operator Davis recorded the following information from a caller: 5.____

Crime:	Rape
Time of Rape:	11:30 A.M.
Place of Rape:	Ralph's Dress Shop, 200 Lexington
Avenue Victim:	Linda Castro - employee at Ralph's Dress Shop
Description of Suspect:	Male, white
Weapon:	Knife

Communications Operator Davis needs to be clear and accurate when relaying information to the patrol car. Which one of the following expresses the above information MOST clearly and accurately?

A. Linda Castro was at 200 Lexington Avenue when she was raped at knife point by a white male. At 11:30 A.M., she is an employee of Ralph's Dress Shop.
B. At 11:30 A.M., Linda Castro reported that she was working in Ralph's Dress Shop located at 200 Lexington Avenue. A white male raped her while she was working at knife point.
C. Linda Castro, an employee of Ralph's Dress Shop, located at 200 Lexington Avenue, reported that at 11:30 A.M. a white male raped her at knife point in the dress shop.
D. At 11:30 A.M., a white male pointed a knife at Linda Castro. He raped an employee of Ralph's Dress Shop, which is located at 200 Lexington Avenue.

Question 6.

DIRECTIONS: Question 6 is to be answered SOLELY on the basis of the following information.

Police Communications Technicians frequently receive low priority calls, which are calls that do not require an immediate police response. When a low priority call is received, the Police Communications Technician should transfer the caller to a tape-recorded message which states *there will be a delay in police response*.

6. Police Communications Technicians should transfer to the low priority taped message a call reporting a 6.____

A. hubcap missing from an auto
B. child has just swallowed poison

C. group of youths fighting with knives
D. woman being assaulted

Questions 7-9.

DIRECTIONS: Questions 7 through 9 are to be answered SOLELY on the basis of the following passage.

On Tuesday, March 20 at 11:55 P.M., Dispatcher Uzel receives a call from a female stating that she immediately needs the police. The dispatcher asks the caller for her address. The excited female answers, *I can not think of it right now.* The dispatcher tries to calm down the caller. At this point, the female caller tells the dispatcher that her address is 1934 Bedford Avenue. The caller then realizes that 1934 Bedford Avenue is her mother's address and gives her address as 3455 Bedford Avenue. Dispatcher Uzel enters the address into the computer and tells the caller that the cross streets are Myrtle and Willoughby Avenues. The caller answers, *I don't live near Willoughby Avenue.* The dispatcher repeats her address at 3455 Bedford Avenue. Then the female states that her name is Linda Harris and her correct address is 5534 Bedford Avenue. Dispatcher Uzel enters the new address into the computer and determines the cross streets to be Utica Avenue and Kings Highway. The caller agrees that these are the cross streets where she lives.

7. What is the caller's CORRECT address? 7.____

A. Unknown
B. 1934 Bedford Avenue
C. 3455 Bedford Avenue
D. 5534 Bedford Avenue

8. What are the cross streets of the correct address? 8.____

A. Myrtle Avenue and Willoughby Avenue
B. Utica Avenue and Kings Highway
C. Bedford Avenue and Myrtle Avenue
D. Utica Avenue and Willoughby Avenue

9. Why did the female caller telephone Dispatcher Uzel? 9.____

A. She needed the cross streets for her address.
B. Her mother needed assistance.
C. The purpose of the call was not mentioned.
D. She did not know where she lived.

Question 10.

DIRECTIONS: Question 10 is to be answered SOLELY on the basis of the following information.

When performing vehicle license plate checks, Operators should do the following in the order given:

I. Request the license plate in question.
II. Repeat the license plate back to the patrol car officers.
III. Check the license plate locally in the computer.
IV. Advise the patrol car officers of the results of the local check.
V. Check the license plate nationally in the computer.
VI. Advise the patrol car officers of the results of the nationwide check.

10. Operator Johnson gets a request from a patrol car officer for a license plate check on a suspicious car. The patrol car officer tells Operator Johnson that the license plate number is XYZ-843, which Operator Johnson repeats back to the patrol car officer. Operator Johnson checks the license plate locally and determines that the car was stolen in the New York City area. 10.____
What should Operator Johnson do NEXT?

A. Repeat the license plate back to patrol car officers.
B. Check the license plate nationally.
C. Advise the patrol car officers of the results of the local check.
D. Advise the patrol ear officers of the results of the nationwide check.

11. Police Communications Technician Hughes receives a call from the owner of The Diamond Dome Jewelry Store, reporting a robbery. He obtains the following information from the caller: 11.____

Place of Occurrence:	The Diamond Dome Jewelry Store, 10 Exchange Place
Time of Occurrence:	10:00 A.M.
Crime:	Robbery of a $50,000 diamond ring
Victim:	Clayton Pelt, owner of The Diamond Dome Jewelry Store
Description of Suspect:	Male, white, black hair, blue suit and gray shirt
Weapon:	Gun

Communications Technician Hughes is about to relay the information to the dispatcher. Which one of the following expresses the above information MOST clearly and accurately?

A. Clayton Pelt reported that at 10:00 A.M. his store, The Diamond Dome Jewelry Store, was robbed at gunpoint. At 10 Exchange Place, a white male with black hair took a $50,000 diamond ring. He was wearing a blue suit and gray shirt.
B. At 10:00 A.M., a black-haired male robbed a $50,000 diamond ring from The Diamond Dome Jewelry Store, which is owned by Clayton Pelt. A white male was wearing a blue suit and gray shirt and had a gun at 10 Exchange Place.
C. At 10:00 A.M., Clayton Pelt, owner of The Diamond Dome Jewelry Store, which is located at 10 Exchange Place, was robbed of a $50,000 diamond ring at gunpoint. The suspect is a white male with black hair wearing a blue suit and gray shirt.
D. In a robbery that occurred at gunpoint, a white male with black hair robbed The Diamond Dome Jewelry Store, which is located at 10 Exchange Place. Clayton Pelt, the owner who was robbed of a $50,000 diamond ring, said he was wearing a blue suit and a gray shirt at 10:00 A.M.

12. Dispatcher Sanders receives the following information from the computer: Place of Occurrence: Bushwick Housing Projects, rear of Building 12B 12.____

Time of Occurrence:	6:00 P.M.
Crime:	Mugging
Victim:	Hispanic female
Suspect:	Unknown

Dispatcher sanders is about to relay the information to the patrol car.
Which one of the following expresses the above information MOST clearly and accurately?

A. In the rear of Building 12B, a Hispanic female was mugged. An unknown suspect was in the Bushwick Housing Projects at 6:00 P.M.
B. At 6:00 P.M., a Hispanic female was mugged by an unknown suspect in the rear of Building 12B, in the Bushwick Housing Projects.
C. At 6:00 P.M., a female is in the rear of Building 12B in the Bushwick Housing Projects. An unknown suspect mugged a Hispanic female.
D. A suspect's identity is unknown in the rear of Building 12B in the Bushwick Housing Project at 6:00 P.M. A Hispanic female was mugged.

Questions 13-15.

DIRECTIONS: Questions 13 through 15 are to be answered SOLELY on the basis of the following passage.

Dispatcher Clark, who is performing a 7:30 A.M. to 3:30 P.M. tour of duty, receives a call from Mrs. Gold. Mrs. Gold states there are four people selling drugs in front of Joe's Cleaners, located at the intersection of Main Street and Broadway. After checking the location in the computer, Dispatcher Clark asks the caller to give a description of each person. She gives the following descriptions: one white male wearing a yellow shirt, green pants, and red sneakers; one Hispanic male wearing a red and white shirt, black pants, and white sneakers; one black female wearing a green and red striped dress and red sandals; and one black male wearing a green shirt, yellow pants, and green sneakers. She also states that the Hispanic male, who is standing near a blue van, has the drugs inside a small black shoulder bag. She further states that she saw the black female hide a gun inside a brown paper bag and place it under a black car parked in front of Joe's Cleaners. The drug selling goes on everyday at various times. During the week, it occurs from 7 A.M. to 1 P.M. and from 5 P.M. to 12 A.M., but on weekends it occurs from 3 P.M. until 7 A.M.

13. Which person was wearing red sneakers? 13.____

A. Black male
B. Hispanic male
C. Black female
D. White male

14. Mrs. Gold stated the drugs were located 14.____

A. under the blue van
B. inside the black shoulder bag
C. under the black car
D. inside the brown paper bag

15. At what time does Mrs. Gold state the drugs are sold on weekends? 15.____

A. 7:30 A.M. - 3:30 P.M.
B. 7:00 A.M. - 1:00 P.M.
C. 5:00 P.M. - 12:00 A.M.
D. 3:00 P.M. - 7:00 A.M.

16. Police Communications Technician Bentley receives a call of an auto being stripped. He obtains the following information from the caller: 16.____

Place of Occurrence:	Corner of West End Avenue and W. 72nd Street
Time of Occurrence:	10:30 P.M.
Witness:	Mr. Simpson
Suspects:	Two white males
Crime:	Auto stripping
Action Taken:	Suspects fled before police arrived

Communications Technician Bentley is about to enter the incident into the computer and send the information to the dispatcher.
Which one of the following expresses the above information MOST clearly and accurately?

A. At 10:30 P.M., Mr. Simpson witnessed two white males stripping an auto parked at the corner of West End Avenue and W. 72nd Street. The suspects fled before the police arrived.
B. An auto was parked at the corner of West End Avenue and W. 72nd Street. Two white males who were stripping at 10:30 P.M. were witnessed by Mr. Simpson. Before the police arrived, the suspects fled.
C. Mr. Simpson saw two white males at the corner of West End Avenue and W. 72nd Street. Fleeing the scene before the police arrived, the witness saw the suspects strip an auto.
D. Before the police arrived at 10:30 P.M. on the corner of West End Avenue and W. 72nd Street, Mr. Simpson witnessed two white males. The suspects, who stripped an auto, fled the scene.

17. 911 Operator Washington receives a call of a robbery and obtains the following information regarding the incident: 17.____

Place of Occurrence:	First National Bank, 45 West 96th Street
Time of Occurrence:	2:55 P.M.
Amount Taken:	$10,000
Description of Suspect:	Male, black, wearing a leather jacket, blue jeans, and white shirt
Weapon:	Gun

911 Operator Washington is about to enter the call into the computer.
Which one of the following expresses the above information MOST clearly and accurately?

A. At 2:55 P.M., the First National Bank, located at 45 West 96th Street, was robbed at gunpoint of $10,000. The suspect is a black male and is wearing a leather jacket, blue jeans, and a white shirt.
B. Ten thousand dollars was robbed from the First National Bank at 2:55 P.M. A black male was wearing a leather jacket, blue jeans, and a white shirt at 45 West 96th Street. He also had a gun.
C. At 2:55 P.M., a male was wearing a leather jacket, blue jeans, and a white shirt. The First National Bank located at 45 West 96th Street was robbed by a black male. Ten thousand dollars was taken at gunpoint.
D. Robbing the First National Bank, a male wore a leather jacket, blue jeans, and a white shirt at gunpoint. A black male was at 45 W. 96th Street. At 2:55 P.M., $10,000 was taken.

Questions 18-20.

DIRECTIONS: Questions 18 through 20 are to be answered SOLELY on the basis of the following passage.

Police Communications Technician Gordon receives a call from a male stating there is a bomb set to explode in the gym of Public School 85 in two hours. Realizing the urgency of the call, the Communications Technician calls the radio dispatcher, who assigns Patrol Car 43A to the scene. Communications Technician Gordon then notifies her supervisor, Miss Smith, who first reviews the tape of the call, then calls the Operations Unit which is notified of all serious incidents, and she reports the facts. The Operations Unit notifies the Mayor's Information Agency and Borough Headquarters of the emergency situation.

18. Who did Communications Technician Gordon notify FIRST? 18.____

A. Supervisor Smith
B. Operations Unit
C. Patrol Car 43A
D. Radio dispatcher

19. The Operations Unit was notified 19.____

A. to inform school personnel of the bomb
B. so they can arrive at the scene before the bomb is scheduled to go off
C. to evacuate the school
D. due to the seriousness of the incident

20. Who did Miss Smith notify? 20.____

A. Patrol Car 43A
B. Operations Unit
C. Mayor's Information Agency
D. Borough Headquarters

KEY (CORRECT ANSWERS)

1.	D	11.	C
2.	C	12.	B
3.	A	13.	D
4.	A	14.	B
5.	C	15.	D
6.	A	16.	A
7.	D	17.	A
8.	B	18.	D
9.	C	19.	D
10.	C	20.	B

TEST 2

DIRECTIONS: Each question or incomplete statement is followed by several suggested answers or completions. Select the one that BEST answers the question or completes the statement. *PRINT THE LETTER OF THE CORRECT ANSWER IN THE SPACE AT THE RIGHT.*

1. A Police Communications Technician receives a call reporting a large gathering. She obtained the following information: 1.____
   Place of Occurrence: Cooper Square Park
   Time of Occurrence: 1:15 A.M.
   Occurrence: Youths drinking and playing loud music
   Complainant: Mrs. Tucker, 20 Cooper Square
   Action Taken: Police scattered the crowd
   Communications Technician Carter is about to relay the information to the dispatcher. Which one of the following expresses the above information MOST clearly and accurately?

   A. The police responded to Cooper Square Park because Mrs. Tucker, who called 911, lives at 20 Cooper Square. The group of youths was scattered due to drinking and playing loud music at 1:15 A.M.
   B. Mrs. Tucker, who lives at 20 Cooper Square, called 911 to make a complaint of a group of youths who were drinking and playing loud music in Cooper Square Park at 1:15 A.M. The police responded and scattered the crowd.
   C. Loud music and drinking in Cooper Square Park by a group of youths caused the police to respond and scatter the crowd. Mrs. Tucker called 911 and complained. At 1:15 A.M., she lives at 20 Cooper Square.
   D. Playing loud music and drinking, Mrs. Tucker called the police. The police scattered a group of youths in Cooper Square Park at 1:15 A.M. Mrs. Tucker lives at 20 Cooper Square.

2. Dispatcher Weston received a call from the owner of a gas station and obtained the following information: 2.____
   Place of Occurrence: Blin's Gas Station, 1800 White Plains Road
   Time of Occurrence: 10:30 A.M.
   Occurrence: Left station without paying
   Witness: David Perilli
   Description of Auto: A white Firebird, license plate GEB275
   Suspect: Male, white, wearing blue jeans and a black T-shirt
   Dispatcher Weston is about to enter the information into the computer.
   Which one of the following expresses the above information MOST clearly and accurately?

   A. At 10:30 A.M., David Perilli witnessed a white male wearing blue jeans and a black T-shirt leave Blin's Gas Station, located at 1800 White Plains Road, without paying. The suspect was driving a white Firebird with license plate GEB275.
   B. Wearing blue jeans and a black T-shirt, David Perilli witnessed a white male leave Blin's Gas Station without paying. He was driving a white Firebird with license plate GEB275. This occurred at 1800 White Plains Road at 10:30 A.M.
   C. David Perilli witnessed a male wearing blue jeans and a black T-shirt driving a white Firebird. At 10:30 A.M., a white male left Blin's Gas Station, located at 1800 White Plains Road, without paying. His license plate was GEB275.

D. At 10:30 A.M., David Perilli witnessed a white male leaving Blin's Gas Station without paying. The driver of a white Firebird, license plate GEB275, was wearing blue jeans and a black T-shirt at 1800 White Plains Road.

Questions 3-4.

DIRECTIONS: Questions 3 and 4 are to be answered SOLELY on the basis of the following information.

Police Communications Technicians are required to assist callers who need non-emergency assistance. The callers are referred to non-emergency agencies. Listed below are some non-emergency situations and the agencies to which they should be referred.

Agency	
Local Precinct	Unoccupied suspicious car
Environmental Protection Agency	Open fire hydrant
Sanitation Department	Abandoned car
S.P.C.A.	Injured, stray or sick animal
Transit Authority	Transit Authority travel information

3. Communications Technician Carter received a call from Mr. Cane, who stated that a car without license plates had been parked in front of his house for five days. Mr. Crane should be referred to the 3.____

   A. A.S.P.C.A.
   B. Transit Authority
   C. Sanitation Department
   D. Environmental Protection Agency

4. Mrs. Dunbar calls to report that a dog has been hit by a car and is lying at the curb in front of her house. Mrs. Dunbar should be referred to the 4.____

   A. Sanitation Department
   B. Local Precinct
   C. Environmental Protection Agency
   D. A.S.P.C.A.

5. Operator Bryant received a call of a robbery and obtained the following information: 5.____

Place of Occurrence:	Deluxe Deli, 303 E. 30th Street
Time of Occurrence:	5:00 P.M.
Crime:	Robbery of $300
Victim:	Bonnie Smith, cashier of Deluxe Deli
Description of Suspect:	White, female, blonde hair, wearing black slacks and a red shirt
Weapon:	Knife

Operator Bryant is about to enter this information into the computer.
Which one of the following expresses the above information MOST clearly and accurately?

A. Bonnie Smith, the cashier of the Deluxe Deli reported at 5:00 P.M. that she was robbed of $300 at knifepoint at 303 East 30th Street. A white female with blonde hair was wearing black slacks and a red shirt.
B. At 5:00 P.M., a blonde-haired female robbed the 303 East 30th Street store. At the Deluxe Deli, cashier Bonnie Smith was robbed of $300 by a white female at knifepoint. She was wearing black slacks and a red shirt.
C. In a robbery that occurred at knifepoint, a blonde-haired white female robbed $300 from the Deluxe Deli. Bonnie Smith, cashier of the 303 East 30th Street store, said she was wearing black slacks and a red shirt at 5:00 P.M.
D. At 5:00 P.M., Bonnie Smith, cashier of the Deluxe Deli, located at 303 East 30th Street, was robbed of $300 at knifepoint. The suspect is a white female with blonde hair wearing black slacks and a red shirt.

6. 911 Operator Landers receives a call reporting a burglary that happened in the past. He obtained the following information from the caller: 6.____

Place of Occurrence:	196 Simpson Street
Date of Occurrence:	June 12
Time of Occurrence:	Between 8:30 A.M. and 7:45 P.M.
Victim:	Mr. Arnold Frank
Items Stolen:	$300 cash, stereo, assorted jewelry, and a VCR

911 Operator Landers is about to enter the incident into the computer.
Which one of the following expresses the above information MOST clearly and accurately?

A. Mr. Arnold Frank stated that on June 12, between 8:30 A.M. and 7:45 P.M., someone broke into his home at 196 Simpson Street and took $300 in cash, a stereo, assorted jewelry, and a VCR.
B. Mr. Arnold Frank stated between 8:30 A.M. and 7:45 P.M., he lives at 196 Simpson Street. A stereo, VCR, $300 in cash, and assorted jewelry were taken on June 12.
C. Between 8:30 A.M. and 7:45 P.M. on June 12, Mr. Arnold Frank reported someone broke into his home. At 196 Simpson Street, a VCR, $300 in cash, a stereo, and assorted jewelry were taken.
D. A stereo, VCR, $300 in cash, and assorted jewelry were taken between 8:30 M. and 7:45 P.M. On June 12, Mr. Arnold Frank reported he lives at 196 Simpson Street.

Questions 7-9.

DIRECTIONS: Questions 7 through 9 are to be answered SOLELY on the basis of the following passage.

Communications Operator Harris receives a call from Mrs. Stein who reports that a car accident occurred in front of her home. She states that one of the cars belongs to her neighbor, Mrs. Brown, and the other car belongs to Mrs. Stein's son, Joseph Stein. Communications Operator Harris enters Mrs. Stein's address into the computer and receives information that no such address exists. She asks Mrs. Stein to repeat her address. Mrs. Stein repeats her address and states that gasoline is leaking from the cars and that smoke is coming from their engines. She further states that people are trapped in the cars and then hangs up.

Communications Operator Harris notifies her supervisor, Jones, that she received a call but was unable to verify the address and that the caller hung up. Mrs. Jones listens to the tape of the call and finds that the caller stated 450 Park Place not 415 Park Place. She advises Communications Operator Harris to enter the correct address, then notify Emergency Service Unit to respond to the individuals trapped in the cars, the Fire Department for the smoke condition, and Emergency Medical Service for any possible injuries.

7. Who did Communications Operator Harris notify concerning the problem with the caller's address? 7.____

   A. Mrs. Brown
   B. Joseph Stein
   C. Joseph Brown
   D. Mrs. Jones

8. Which agency was Communications Operator Harris advised to notify concerning individuals trapped in the cars? 8.____

   A. Emergency Medical Service
   B. Fire Department
   C. Emergency Service Unit
   D. NYC Police Department

9. Which agency did Supervisor Jones advise Communications Operator Harris to notify for the smoke condition? 9.____

   A. NYC Police Department
   B. Emergency Medical Service
   C. Fire Department
   D. Emergency Service Unit

Question 10.

DIRECTIONS: Question 10 is to be answered SOLELY on the basis of the following information.

When a Police Communications Technician receives a call concerning a bank robbery, a Communications Technician should do the following in the order given:

I. Get address and name of the bank from the caller.
II. Enter the address into the computer.
III. Use the *Hotline* button to alert the dispatcher of the serious incident going into the computer.
IV. Get back to the caller and get the description of the suspect and other pertinent information.
V. Enter additional information into the computer and send it to the dispatcher.
VI. Upgrade the seriousness of the incident so it appears first on dispatcher's screen.
VII. Notify the Supervising Police Communications Technician of the bank robbery.

10. Police Communications Technician Brent receives a call from Mr. Ross stating that while he was on line at the Trust Bank, at West 34th Street and 9th Avenue, he witnessed a bank robbery. Communications Technician Brent enters the address into the computer, then presses the *Hotline* button and alerts the dispatcher that there was a bank robbery at the Trust Bank on West 34th Street and 9th Avenue. Mr. Ross continues to state that the robber is a white male in his 30's wearing a light blue shirt and blue jeans. After obtaining other pertinent information, the NEXT step Communications Technician Brent should take is to 10.____

A. enter additional information into the computer and send it to the dispatcher
B. upgrade the seriousness of the incident so it appears first on the dispatcher's screen
C. notify his supervisor of the bank robbery
D. use the *Hotline* button to alert the dispatcher of a serious incident going into the computer

11. Dispatcher Wilson receives a call regarding drugs being sold in the lobby of an apartment building. He obtains the following information: 11.____

Place of Occurrence:	305 Willis Avenue
Time of Occurrence:	2:00 P.M.
Witnesses:	Roy Rodriguez and Harry Armstrong
Suspect:	Melvin Talbot, left the scene before the police arrived
Crime:	Drug sale

Dispatcher Wilson is about to enter this incident into the computer.
Which one of the following expresses the above information MOST clearly and accurately?

A. Roy Rodriguez and Harry Armstrong reported that they witnessed Melvin Talbot selling drugs in the lobby of 305 Willis Avenue at 2:00 P.M. The suspect left the scene before the police arrived.
B. In the lobby, Roy Rodriguez reported at 2:00 P.M. he saw Melvin Talbot selling drugs with Harry Armstrong. He left the lobby of 305 Willis Avenue before the police arrived.
C. Roy Rodriguez and Harry Armstrong witnessed drugs being sold at 305 Willis Avenue. Before the police arrived at 2:00 P.M., Melvin Talbot left the lobby.
D. Before the police arrived, witnesses stated that Melvin Talbot was selling drugs. At 305 Willis Avenue, in the lobby, Roy Rodriguez and Harry Armstrong said he left the scene at 2:00 P.M.

12. Operator Rogers receives a call of a car being stolen. He obtains the following information: 12.____

Place of Occurrence:	Parking lot at 1723 East 20th Street
Time of Occurrence:	2:30 A.M.
Vehicle Involved:	1988 Toyota Corolla
Suspects:	Male, Hispanic, wearing a red T-shirt
Crime:	Auto theft
Witness:	Janet Alonzo

Operator Rogers is entering the information into the computer.
Which one of the following expresses the above information MOST clearly and accurately?

A. At 2:30 A.M., wearing a red T-shirt, Janet Alonzo witnessed a 1988 Toyota Corolla being stolen by a male Hispanic in the parking lot at 1723 East 20th Street.
B. A male Hispanic, wearing a red T-shirt, was in the parking lot at 1723 East 20th Street." At 2:30 A.M., Janet Alonzo witnessed a 1988 Toyota Corolla being stolen.
C. At 2:30 A.M., Janet Alonzo witnessed a 1988 Toyota Corolla in the parking lot at 1723 East 20th Street being stolen by a male Hispanic who is wearing a red T-shirt.
D. Janet Alonzo witnessed a 1988 Toyota Corolla in the parking lot being stolen. At 2:30 A.M., a male Hispanic was wearing a red T-shirt at 1723 East 20th Street.

Question 13.

DIRECTIONS: Question 13 is to be answered SOLELY on the basis of the following information.

There are times when Police Communications Technicians have to reassign officers in a patrol car from a less serious incident which does not require immediate police response to an incident of a more serious nature which does require immediate police response. Police Communications Technicians must choose among the assigned patrol cars and determine which one is assigned to the least serious incident, then reassign that one to the situation which requires immediate police response.

Communications Technician Reese is working the 13th Division which covers the 79th Precinct. There are only four patrol cars working in the 79th Precinct. They are assigned as follows:

79A is assigned to a car accident with injuries involving an intoxicated driver.

79B is assigned to a group of teenagers playing loud music in a park.

79C is assigned to a group of teenagers trying to steal liquor in a liquor store, who are possibly armed with guns.

79D is assigned to a suspicious man in a bank, with possible intentions to rob the bank.

13. If Communications Technician Reese receives a call of an incident that requires immediate police response, which patrol car should be reassigned? 13.____

A. 79A B. 79B C. 79C D. 79D

Questions 14-16.

DIRECTIONS: Questions 14 through 16 are to be answered SOLELY on the basis of the following information.

On May 12, at 3:35 P.M., Police Communications Technician Connor receives a call from a child caller requesting an ambulance for her mother, whom she cannot wake. The child did not know her address, but gave Communications Technician Connor her apartment number and telephone number. Communications Technician Connor's supervisor, Ms. Bendel, is advised of the situation and consult's Cole's Directory, a listing published by the Bell Telephone Company, to obtain an address when only the telephone number is known. The telephone number is unlisted. Ms. Bendel asks Communications Technician Taylor to call Telco Security to obtain an address from their telephone number listing. Communications Technician Taylor speaks to Ms. Morris of Telco Security and obtains the address. Communications Technician Connor, who is still talking with the child, is given the address by Communications Technician Taylor. She enters the information into the computer system and transfers the caller to the Emergency Medical Service.

14. What information did Communications Technician Connor obtain from the child caller? 14.____

A. Telephone number and apartment number
B. Name and address
C. Address and telephone number
D. Apartment number and address

15. Communications Technician Taylor obtained the address from 15.____

A. Communications Technician Connor
B. Ms. Morris
C. Supervisor Bendel
D. the child caller

16. The caller's address was obtained by calling 16.____

A. Cole's Directory
B. Telco Security
C. Emergency Medical Service
D. The Telephone Company

Question 17.

DIRECTIONS: Question 17 is to be answered SOLELY on the basis of the following information.

The following incidents appear on the Police Communications Technician's computer screen which were called in by three different callers at the same time:

I. At 3040 Hill Avenue between Worth and Centre Streets, there are two people fighting in the third floor hallway. One of them has a shiny metal object.
II. In a building located on Hill Avenue between Worth and Centre Streets, a man and a woman are having an argument on the third floor. The woman has a knife in her hand.
III. In front of Apartment 3C on the third floor, a husband and wife are yelling at each other. The wife is pointing a metal letter opener at her husband. The building is located on the corner of Hill Avenue and Worth Street.

17. A Police Communications Technician may be required to combine into one incident many calls that appear on the computer screen if they seem to be reporting the same incident. Which of the above should a Police Communications Technician combine into one incident? 17.____

A. I and II
B. I and III
C. II and III
D. I, II, and III

Questions 18-19.

DIRECTIONS: Questions 18 and 19 are to be answered SOLELY on the basis of the following information.

Police Communications Technicians must be able to identify and assign codes to the crimes described in the calls they receive. All crimes are coded by number and by priority. The priority code number indicates the seriousness of the crime. The lower the priority number, the more serious the crime.

Listed below is a chart of several crimes and their definitions. The corresponding crime code and priority code number are given.

CRIME	DEFINITION	CRIME CODE	PRIORITY CODE
Criminal Mischief:	Occurs when a person intentionally damages another person's property	29	6
Harrassment:	Occurs when a person intentionally annoys another person by striking, shoving, or kicking them without causing injury	27	8
Aggravated Harrassment:	Occurs when a person intentionally annoys another person by using any form of communication	28	9
Theft of Service:	Occurs when a person intentionally avoids payment for services given	25	7

18. Communications Technician Rogers received a call from Mrs. Freeman, who stated that her next door neighbor, whom she had an argument with, has thrown a rock through her apartment window. 18.____
Which one of the following is the CORRECT crime code?

A. 29 B. 28 C. 27 D. 25

19. Communications Technician Tucker received a call from a man who stated that he is a waiter at the Frontier Diner. He states that one of his customers was refusing to pay for his meal. 19.____
Which one of the following is the CORRECT priority code number for this crime?

A. 6 B. 7 C. 8 D. 9

Dispatcher Matthews received a call of a bomb threat. He obtained the following information; 19.____

Address of Occurrence: 202 Church Avenue
Location: 2nd floor men's room
Time of Call: 12:00 P.M.
Time of Occurrence: 2:00 P.M.
Terrorist Organization: People *Against Government*

Caller: Anonymous male member of *People* Against Government
Action Taken: Supervisor Jones notified of the bomb threat

Dispatcher Matthews is about to enter the information into the computer.

Which one of the following expresses the above information MOST clearly and accurately?

A. An anonymous male called Dispatcher Matthews and told him that a bomb is set to go off at 202 Church Avenue in the 2nd floor men's room at 2:00 P.M. Dispatcher Matthews notified Supervisor Jones that the caller is from *People Against Government* at 12:00 P.M.

B. Dispatcher Matthews received a call in the 2nd floor men's room of a bomb threat from an anonymous male member of the *People Against Government* terrorist organization. He notified Supervisor Jones at 12:00 P.M. that a bomb is set to go off at 2:00 P.M. at 202 Church Avenue.

C. Dispatcher Matthews received a call at 202 Church Avenue from the *People Against Government,* a terrorist organization. An anonymous male stated that a bomb is set to go off at 2:00 P.M. in the 2nd floor men's room. At 12:00 P.M., Dispatcher Matthews notified Supervisor Jones of the call.

D. At 12:00 P.M., Dispatcher Matthews received a call from an anonymous male caller who states that he is from a terrorist organization known as *People Against Government.* He states that a bomb has been placed in the 2nd floor men's room of 202 Church Avenue and is set to go off at 2:00 P.M. Dispatcher Matthews notified Supervisor Jones of the bomb threat.

KEY (CORRECT ANSWERS)

1.	B	11.	A
2.	A	12.	C
3.	C	13.	B
4.	D	14.	A
5.	D	15.	B
6.	A	16.	B
7.	D	17.	D
8.	C	18.	A
9.	C	19.	B
10.	A	20.	D

EXAMINATION SECTION

TEST 1

DIRECTIONS: Each question or incomplete statement is followed by several suggested answers or completions. Select the one that BEST answers the question or completes the statement. *PRINT THE LETTER OF THE CORRECT ANSWER IN THE SPACE AT THE RIGHT.*

1. You are operating the switchboard and you receive an outside call for an extension line which is busy. 1.____
The one of the following which you should do FIRST is to
   A. ask the caller to try again later
   B. ask the caller to wait and inform him every thirty seconds about the status of the extension line
   C. tell the caller the line is busy and ask him if he wishes to wait
   D. tell the caller the line is busy and that you will connect him as soon as possible

2. A person comes to your work area. He makes comments which make no sense, gives foolish opinions, and tells you that he has enemies who are after him. He appears to be mentally ill. 2.____
Of the following, the FIRST action to take is to
   A. humor him by agreeing and sympathize with him
   B. try to reason with him and point out that his fears or opinions are unfounded
   C. have him arrested immediately
   D. tell him to leave at once

3. You are speaking with someone on the telephone who asks you a question which you cannot answer. You estimate that you can probably obtain the requested information in about five minutes. 3.____
Of the following, the MOST appropriate course of action would be to tell the caller that
   A. the information will take a short while to obtain, and then ask her for her name and number so that you can call her back when you have the information
   B. the information is available now, but she should call back later
   C. you do not know the answer and refer her to another division you think might be of service
   D. she is being placed on *hold* and that you will be with her in about five minutes

4. A person with a very heavy foreign accent comes to your work area and starts talking to you. He is very excited and is speaking too rapidly for you to understand what he is saying. 4.____
Of the following, the FIRST action for you to take is to

A. refer the person to your supervisor
B. continue your work and ignore the person in the hope that he will be discouraged and leave the building
C. ask or motion to the person to speak more slowly and have him repeat what he is trying to communicate
D. assume that the person is making a complaint, tell him that his problem will be taken care of, and then go back to your work

5. Assume that you are responsible for handling supplies. You notice that you are running low on a particular type of manila file folder exceptionally fast. You believe that someone in the precinct is taking the folders for other than official use. 5.____
In this situation, the one of the following that you should do FIRST is to
A. put up a notice stating that supplies have been disappearing and ask for the staff's cooperation in eliminating the problem
B. speak to your supervisor about the matter and let him decide on a course of action
C. watch the supply cabinet to determine who is taking the folders
D. ignore the situation and put in a requisition for additional folders

6. One afternoon, several of the officers ask you to perform different tasks. Each task requires a half day of work. Each officer tells you that his assignment must be finished by 4 P.M. the next day. 6.____
Of the following, the BEST way to handle this situation is to
A. do the assignments as quickly as you can, in the order in which the officers handed them to you
B. do some work on each assignment in the order of the ranks of the assigning officers and hand in as much as you are able to finish
C. speak to your immediate supervisor in order to determine the priority of assignments
D. accept all four assignments but explain to the last officer that you may not be able to finish his job

7. Every morning, several officers congregate around your work station during their breaks. You find their conversations very distracting. 7.____
The one of the following which you should do FIRST is to
A. ask them to cooperate with you by taking their breaks somewhere else
B. concentrate as best you can because their breaks do not last very long
C. reschedule your break to coincide with theirs
D. tell your supervisor that the officers are very uncooperative

8. One evening when you are very busy, you answer the phone and find that you are speaking with one of the neighborhood cranks, an elderly man who constantly complains that his neighbors are noisy. 8.____
In this situation, the MOST appropriate action for you to take is to
A. hang up and go on with your work
B. note the complaint and process it in the usual way
C. tell the man that his complaint will be investigated and then forget about it
D. tell the man that you are very buy and ask him to call back later

9. One morning you answer a telephone call for Lieutenant Jones, who is busy on another line. You inform the caller that Lieutenant Jones is on another line and this party says he will hold. After two minutes, Lieutenant Jones is still speaking on the first call. 9.____
Of the following, the FIRST thing for you to do is to
   A. ask the second caller whether it is an emergency
   B. signal Lieutenant Jones to let him know there is another call waiting for him
   C. request that the second caller try again later
   D. inform the second caller that Lieutenant Jones' line is still busy

10. The files in your office have been overcrowded and difficult to work with since you started working there. One day your supervisor is transferred and another aide in your office decides to discard three drawers of the oldest materials. 10.____
For him to take this action is
   A. *desirable*; it will facilitate handling the more active materials
   B. *undesirable*; no file should be removed from its point of origin
   C. *desirable*; there is no need to burden a new supervisor with unnecessary information
   D. *undesirable*; no file should be discarded without first noting what material has been discarded

11. You have been criticized by the lieutenant-in-charge because of spelling errors in some of your typing. You have only copied the reports as written, and you realize that the errors occurred in work given to you by Sergeant X. 11.____
Of the following, the BEST way for you to handle this situation is to
   A. tell the lieutenant that the spelling errors are Sergeant X's, not yours, because they occur only when you type his reports
   B. tell the lieutenant that you only type the reports as given to you, without implicating anyone
   C. inform Sergeant X that you have been unjustly criticized because of his spelling errors and politely request that he be more careful in the future
   D. use a dictionary whenever you have doubt regarding spelling

12. You have recently found several items misfiled. You believe that this occurred because a new administrative aide in your section has been making mistakes. 12.____
The BEST course of action for you to take is to
   A. refile the material and say nothing about it
   B. send your supervisor an anonymous note of complaint about the filing errors
   C. show the errors to the new administrative aide and tell him why they are errors in filing
   D. tell your supervisor that the new administrative aide makes a lot of errors in filing

13. One of your duties is to record information on a standard printed form regarding missing cars. One call you receive concerns a custom-built auto which has apparently been stolen. There seems to be no place on the form for many of the details which the owner gives you. 13.____

Of the following, the BEST way for you to obtain an adequate description of this car would be to

A. complete the form as best you can and attach another sheet containing the additional information the owner gives you
B. complete the form as best you can and request that the owner submit a photograph of the missing car
C. scrap the form since it is inadequate in this case and make out a report based on the information the owner gives you
D. complete the form as best you can and ignore extraneous information that the form does not call for

14. One weekend, you develop a painful infection in one hand. You know that your typing speed will be much slower than normal, and the likelihood of your making mistakes will be increased. 14.____
Of the following, the BEST course of action for you to take in this situation is to

A. report to work as scheduled and do your typing assignments as best you can without complaining
B. report to work as scheduled and ask your co-workers to divide your typing assignments until your hand heals
C. report to work as scheduled and ask your supervisor for non-typing assignments until your hand heals
D. call in sick and remain on medical leave until your hand is completely healed so that you can perform your normal duties

15. When filling out a departmental form during an interview concerning a citizen complaint, an administrative aide should know the purpose of each question that he asks the citizen. 15.____
For such information to be supplied by the department is

A. *advisable*, because the aide may lose interest in the job if he is not fully informed about the questions he has to ask
B. *inadvisable*, because the aide may reveal the true purpose of the questions to the citizens
C. *advisable*, because the aide might otherwise record superficial or inadequate answers if he does not fully understand the questions
D. *inadvisable*, because the information obtained through the form may be of little importance to the aide

16. Which one of the following is NOT a general accepted rule of telephone etiquette for an administrative aide? 16.____

A. Answer the telephone as soon as possible after the first ring
B. Speak in a louder than normal tone of voice, on the assumption that the caller is hard-of-hearing
C. Have a pencil and paper ready at all times with which to make notes and take messages
D. Use the tone of your voice to give the caller the impression of cooperativeness and willingness to be of service

17. The one of the following which is the BEST reason for placing the date and time of receipt of incoming mail is that this procedure 17.____
    A. aids the filing of correspondence in alphabetical order
    B. fixes responsibility for promptness in answering correspondence
    C. indicates that the mail has been checked for the presence of a return address
    D. makes it easier to distribute the mail in sequence

18. Which one of the following is the FIRST step that you should take when filing a document by subject? 18.____
    A. Arrange related documents by date with the latest date in front
    B. Check whether the document has been released for filing
    C. Cross-reference the document if necessary
    D. Determine the category under which the document will be filed

19. The one of the following which is NOT generally employed to keep tract of frequently used material requiring future attention is a 19.____
    A. card tickler file
    B. dated follow-up folder
    C. periodic transferral of records
    D. signal folder

20. Assume that a newly appointed administrative aide arrives 15 minutes late for the start of his tour of duty. One of his co-workers tells him not to worry because he has signed him in on time. The co-worker assures him that he would be willing to over for him anytime he is late and hopes the aide will do the same for him. The aide agrees to do so. 20.____
    This arrangement is
    A. *desirable*; it prevents both men from getting a record for tardiness
    B. *undesirable*; signing in for each other is dishonest
    C. *desirable*; cooperation among co-workers is an important factor in morale
    D. *undesirable*; they will get caught if one is held up in a lengthy delay

21. An administrative aide takes great pains to help a citizen who approaches him with a problem. The citizen thanks the aide curtly and without enthusiasm. 21.____
    Under these circumstances, it would be MOST courteous for the aide to
    A. tell the citizen he was glad to be of service
    B. ask the citizen to put the compliment into writing and send it to his supervisor
    C. tell the citizen just what pains he took to render this service so that the citizen will be fully aware of his efforts
    D. make no reply and ignore the citizen's remarks

22. Assume that your supervisor spends a week training you, a newly appointed administrative aide, to sort fingerprint for filing purposes. After doing this type of filing for several day, you get an idea which you believe would improve upon the method in use. 22.____
    Of the following, the BEST action for you to take in this situation is to
    A. wait to see whether your idea still look good after you have had more experience
    B. try your idea out before bringing it up with your supervisor

C. discuss your idea with your supervisor
D. forget about this idea since the fingerprint sorting system was devised by experts

23. Which one of the following is NOT a useful filing practice? 23.____
A. Filing active records in the most accessible parts of the file cabinet
B. Filling a file drawer to capacity in order to save space
C. Gluing small documents to standard-size paper before filing
D. Using different colored tab for various filing categories

24. A citizen comes in to make a complaint to an administrative aide. 24.____
The one of the following action which would be the MOST serious example of discourtesy would be for the aide to
A. refuse to look up from his desk even though he knows someone is waiting to speak to him
B. not use the citizen's name when addressing him once his identity has been ascertained
C. interrupt the citizen's story to ask questions
D. listen to the complaint and refer the citizen to a special office

25. Suppose that one of your neighbors walks into the precinct where you are an administrative aide and asks you to make 100 copies of a letter on the office duplicating machine for his personal use. 25.____
Of the following, what action should you take FIRST in this situation?
A. Pretend that you do not know the person and order him to leave the building
B. Call a police officer and report the person for attempting to make illegal use of police equipment
C. Tell the person that you will copy the letter but only when you are off-duty
D. Explain to the person that you cannot use police equipment for non-police work

KEY (CORRECT ANSWERS)

1. C
2. A
3. A
4. C
5. B

6. C
7. A
8. B
9. D
10. D

11. D
12. C
13. A
14. C
15. C

16. B
17. B
18. B
19. C
20. B

21. A
22. C
23. B
24. A
25. D

TEST 2

DIRECTIONS: Each question or incomplete statement is followed by several suggested answers or completions. Select the one that BEST answers the question or completes the statement. *PRINT THE LETTER OF THE CORRECT ANSWER IN THE SPACE AT THE RIGHT.*

Questions 1-6.

DIRECTIONS: Questions 1 through 6 are to be answered on the basis of the information supplied in the chart below.

LAW ENFORCEMENT OFFICERS KILLED
(By Type of Activity)
2012-2021

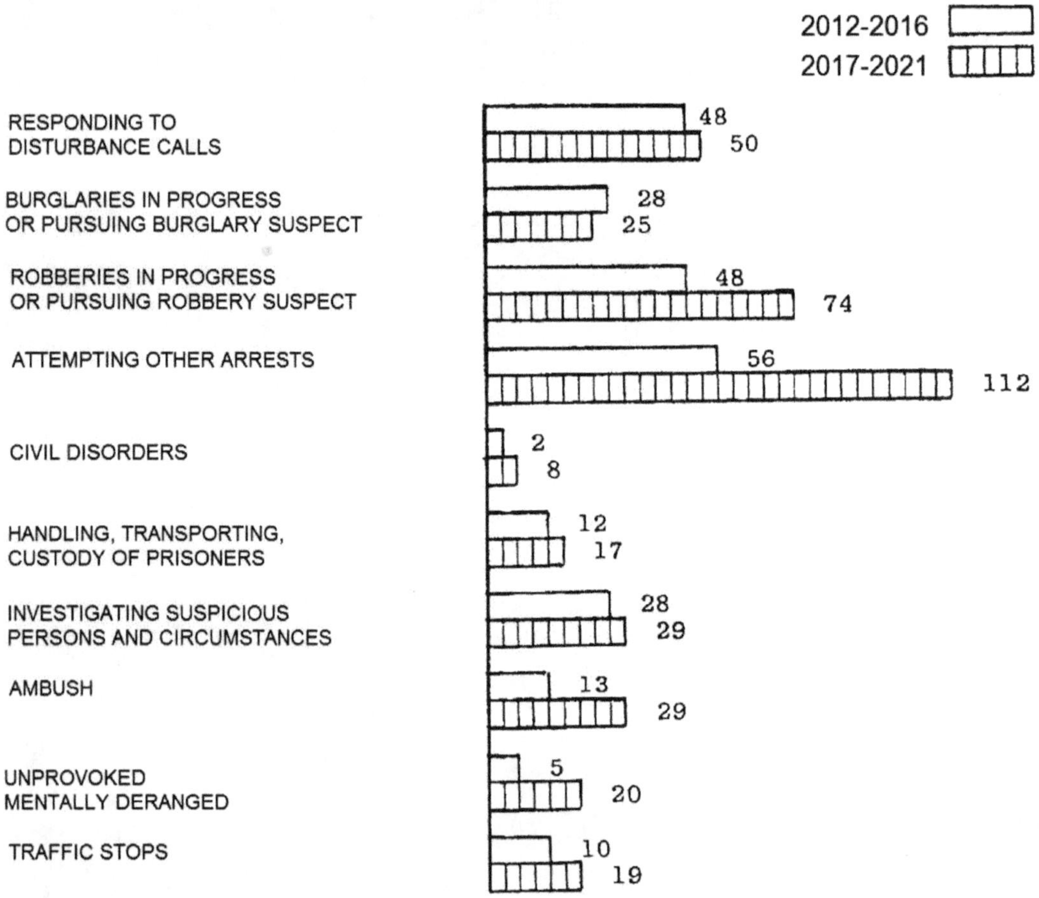

1. According to the above chart, the percent of the total number of law enforcement officers killed from 2012-2021 in activities related to burglaries and robberies is MOST NEARLY _____ percent. 1.____
   A. 8.4 B. 19.3 C. 27.6 D. 36.2

2. According to the above chart, the two of the following categories which increased from 2012–16 to 2017–21 by the same percent are 2.____
   A. ambush and traffic stops
   B. attempting other arrests and ambush
   C. civil disorders and unprovoked mentally deranged
   D. response to disturbance calls and investigating suspicious persons and circumstances

3. According to the above chart, the percentage increase in law enforcement officers killed from the 2012-16 period to the 2017-21 period is MOST NEARLY _____ percent. 3.____
   A. 34 B. 53 C. 65 D. 100

4. According to the above chart, in which one of the following activities did the number of law enforcement officers killed increase by 100 percent? 4.____
   A. Ambush
   B. Attempting other arrests
   C. Robberies in progress or pursuing robbery suspect
   D. Traffic stops

5. According to the above chart, the two of the following activities during which the total number of law enforcement officers killed from 2012 to 2021 was the same are 5.____
   A. burglaries in progress or pursuing burglary suspect and investigating suspicious persons and circumstances
   B. handling, transporting, custody of prisoner and traffic stops
   C. investigating suspicious persons and circumstances and ambush
   D. responding to disturbance calls and robberies in progress or pursuing robbery suspect

6. According to the categories in the above chart, the one of the following statements which can be made about law enforcement officers killed from 2012 to 2016 is that 6.____
   A. the number of law enforcement officers killed during civil disorders equals one-sixth of the number killed responding to disturbance calls
   B. the number of law enforcement officers killed during robberies in progress or pursuing robbery suspect equals 25 percent of the number killed while handling or transporting prisoners
   C. the number of law enforcement officers killed during traffic stops equals one-half the number killed for unprovoked reasons or by the mentally deranged
   D. twice as many law enforcement officers were killed attempting other arrests as were killed during burglaries in progress or pursuing burglary suspect

Questions 7-10.

DIRECTIONS: Assume that all arrests fall into two mutually exclusive categories, felonies and misdemeanors. Last week 620 arrests were made in Precinct A, of which 403 were for felonies. Questions 7 through 10 are to be answered on the basis of this information.

7. The percent of all arrests made in Precinct A last week which were for felonies was _____ percent. 7.____
   A. 55 B. 60 C. 65 D. 70

8. If 3/5 of all persons arrested for felonies and 1/4 of all persons arrested for misdemeanors were carrying weapons, then the number of arrests involving persons carrying weapons in Precinct A last week was MOST NEARLY 8.____
   A. 135 B. 295 C. 415 D. 525

9. If five times as many men as women were arrested for felonies, and half as many women as men were arrested for misdemeanors, then the number of women arrested in Precinct A last week was APPROXIMATELY 9.____
   A. 90 B. 120 C. 175 D. 210

10. If the ratio of arrests made on weekends (Friday through Sunday) to arrests made on weekdays (Monday through Thursday) is 2:1, then the number of arrests made in Precinct A last weekend was 10.____
    A. 308 B. 340 C. 372 D. 413

11. The police precincts covering the county receive calls at the average rate of two per minute during the 8 A.M. to 4 P.M. tour, but this rate increases by 50 percent during the 4 P.M. to 12 A.M. tour. However, the initial rate decreases by 50 percent during the 12 A.M. to 8 A.M. tour. 11.____
    The number of calls received by the precincts covering the county on this basis is one 24-hour day is
    A. 960 B. 1,440 C. 2,880 D. 3,360

12. If an administrative aide is expected to handle 15 calls per hour and Precinct C averages 840 calls during the 4 P.M. to 12 A.M. tour, then the number of aides needed in Precinct C to handle calls during this tour is 12.____
    A. 4 B. 5 C. 6 D. 7

13. If in a group of ten administrative aides, four type 40 words per minute, one types 45, two type 50, two type 60, and one types 65, then the average speed in the group is 13.____
    A. 49 B. 50 C. 51 D. 52

14. An administrative aide works from midnight to 8 A.M. on a certain day and then is off for 64 hours. 14.____
    He is due back at work at
    A. 8 A.M. B. 12 noon C. 4 P.M. D. 12 midnight

15. If a certain aide take one hour to type 2 accident reports or 6 missing person reports, then the length of time he will require to finish 7 accident reports and 15 missing persons reports is _____ hours _____ minutes. 15.____
    A. 6; 0 B. 6; 30 C. 8; 0 D. 8; 40

16. If one administrative aide can alphabetize 320 reports per hour and another can do 280 per hour, then the number of reports that both could alphabetize during an 8-hour tour is 16.____
    A. 4,800 B. 5,200 C. 5,400 D. 5,700

17. If 1,000 candidates applied for administrative aide, and out of those applying 7/8 appear for the written test, and out of those who take the written test 66 2/4 percent pass it, and out of those who pass the written test 85 percent pass the medical exam, then the number of candidates still eligible to become administrative aides will be about 17.____
    A. 245 B. 495 C. 585 D. 745

18. If the number of murders in the city in 2018 was 415, and the number of murders has increased by 8 percent each year since that year, then in 2021 we would expect the number of murders to be about 18.____
    A. 484 B. 523 C. 548 D. 565

19. If a person reported missing on April 15 was found murdered on July 4, how many days was he missing? (Include April 15 but NOT July 4 in the total.) 19.____
    A. 76 B. 80 C. 82 D. 84

20. Suppose that a pile of 96 file cards measures one inch in height and that it takes you ½ hour to file these cards away.
    If you are given three piles of cards which measure 2½ inches high, 1¾ inches high, and $3^3/_8$ inches high, respectfully, the time it would take to file the cards is MOST NEARLY _____ hours and _____ minutes. 20.____
    A. 2; 30 B. 3; 50 C. 6; 45 D. 8; 15

Questions 21-30.

DIRECTIONS: Questions 21 through 30 test how good you are at catching mistakes in typing or printing. In each question, the name and addresses in Column II should be an exact copy of the name and address in Column I.
Mark your answer:
A. if there is no mistake in either name or address
B. if there is a mistake in both name and address
C. if there is a mistake only in the name
D. if there is a mistake only in the address

	COLUMN I	COLUMN II	
21.	Milos Yanocek 33-60 14 Street Long Island City, NY 11011	Milos Yanocek 33-60 14 Street Long Island City, NY 11001	21.____

22.	Alphonse Sabattelo 24 Minnetta Lane New York, NY 10006	Alphonse Sabbattelo 24 Minetta Lane New York, NY 10006	22.____
23.	Helen Stearn 5 Metroplitan Oval Bronx, NY 10462	Helene Steam 5 Metropolitan Oval Bronx, NY 10462	23.____
24.	Jacob Weisman 231 Francis Lewis Boulevard Forest Hills, NY 11325	Jacob Weisman 231 Francis Lewis Boulevard Forest Hill, NY 11325	24.____
25.	Riccardo Fuente 135 West 83 Street New York, NY 10024	Riccardo Fuentes 134 West 88 Street New York, NY 10024	25.____
26.	Dennis Lauber 52 Avenue D Brooklyn, NY 11216	Dennis Lauder 52 Avenue D Brooklyn, NY 11216	26.____
27.	Paul Cutter 195 Galloway Avenue Staten Island, NY 10356	Paul Cutter 175 Galloway Avenue Staten Island, NY 10365	27.____
28.	Sean Donnelly 45-58 41 Avenue Woodside, NY 11168	Sean Donnelly 45-58 41 Avenue Woodside, NY 11168	28.____
29.	Clyde Willot 1483 Rockaway Avenue Brooklyn, NY 11238	Clyde Willat 1483 Rockaway Avenue Brooklyn, NY 11238	29.____
30.	Michael Stanakis 419 Sheriden Avenue Staten Island, NY 10363	Michael Stanakis 419 Sheraden Avenue Staten Island, NY 10363	30.____

Questions 31-40.

DIRECTIONS: Questions 31 through 40 are to be answered SOLELY on the basis of the following information.

Column I consists of serial numbers of dollar bills. Column II shows different ways of arranging the corresponding serial numbers.

The serial numbers of dollar bills in Column I begin and end with a capital letter and have an eight-digit number in between. The serial numbers in Column I are to be arranged according to the following rules:

First: In alphabetical order according to the first letter.
Second: When two or more serial numbers have the same first letter, in alphabetical order according to the last letter.
Third: When two or more serial numbers have the same first and last letters, in numerical order, beginning with the lowest number.

The serial numbers in Column I are numbered (1) through (5) in the order in which they are listed. In Column II, the numbers (1) through (5) are arranged in four different ways to show different arrangements of the corresponding serial numbers. Choose the answer in Column II in which the serial numbers are arranged according to the above rules.
SAMPLE QUESTION:

COLUMN I	COLUMN II
(1) E75044127B	(A) 4, 1, 3, 2, 5
(2) B96399104A	(B) 4, 1 2, 3, 5
(3) B93939086A	(C) 4, 3, 2 5, 1
(4) B47064465H	(D) 3, 2, 5, 4, 1
(5) B99040922A	

In the sample question, the four serial numbers starting with B should be put before the serial numbers starting with E. The serial numbers starting with B and ending with A should be put before the serial number starting with B and ending with H. The three serial numbers starting with B and ending with A should be listed in numerical order, beginning with the lowest number. The correct way to arrange the serial numbers, therefore, is
(3) B93939086A
(2) B96399104A
(5) B99040922A
(4) B47064465H
(1) B75044127B

Since the order of arrangement is 3, 2, 5, 4, 1, the answer to the sample question is (D).

	COLUMN I	COLUMN II	
31.	(1) P44343324Y	A. 2, 3, 1, 4, 5	31.____
	(2) P44141341S	B. 1, 5, 3, 2, 4	
	(3) P44141431L	C. 4, 2, 3, 5, 1	
	(4) P41143413W	D. 5, 3, 2, 4, 1	
	(5) P44313433H		
32.	(1) D89077275M	A. 3, 2, 5, 3, 1	32.____
	(2) D98073724N	B. 1, 4, 3, 2, 5	
	(3) D90877274N	C. 4, 1, 5, 2, 3	
	(4) D98877275M	D. 1, 3, 2, 5, 3	
	(5) D98873725N		

33. (1) H32548137E (2) H35243178A (3) H35284378F (4) H35288337A (5) H32883173B
A. 2, 4, 5, 1, 3
B. 1, 5, 2, 3, 4
C. 1, 5, 2, 4, 3
D. 2, 1, 5, 3, 4
33.____

34. (1) K24165039H (2) F24106599A (3) L21406639G (4) C24156093A (5) K24165593D
A. 4, 2, 5, 3, 1
B. 2, 3, 4, 1, 5
C. 4, 2, 5, 1, 3
D. 1, 3, 4, 5, 2
34.____

35. (1) H79110642E (2) H79101928E (3) A79111567F (4) H79111796E (5) A79111618F
A. 2, 1, 3, 5, 4
B. 2, 1, 4, 5, 3
C. 3, 5, 2, 1, 4
D. 4, 3, 5, 1, 2
35.____

36. (1) P16388385W (2) R16388335V (3) P16383835W (4) R18386865V (5) P18686865W
A. 3, 4, 5, 2, 1
B. 2, 3, 4, 5, 1
C. 2, 4, 3, 1, 5
D. 3, 1, 5, 2, 4
36.____

37. (1) B42271749G (2) B42271779G (3) E43217779G (4) B42874119C (5) E42817749G
A. 4, 1, 5, 2, 3
B. 4, 1, 2, 5, 3
C. 1, 2, 4, 5, 3
D. 5, 3, 1, 2, 4
37.____

38. (1) M57906455S (2) N87077758S (3) N87707757B (4) M57877759B (5) M57906555S
A. 4, 1, 5, 3, 2
B. 3, 4, 1, 5, 2
C. 4, 1, 5, 2, 3
D. 1, 5, 3, 2, 4
38.____

39. (1) C69336894Y (2) C69336684V (3) C69366887W (4) C69366994Y (5) C69336865V
A. 2, 5, 3, 1, 4
B. 3, 2, 5, 1, 4
C. 3, 1, 4, 5, 2
D. 2, 5, 1, 3, 4
39.____

40. (1) A56247181D (2) A56272128P (3) H56247128D (4) H56272288P (5) A56247188D
A. 1, 5, 3, 2, 4
B. 3, 1, 5, 2, 4
C. 3, 2, 1, 5, 4
D. 1, 5, 2, 3, 4
40.____

Questions 41-48.

DIRECTIONS: Questions 41 through 48 are to be answered SOLELY on the basis of the following passage.

Auto theft is prevalent and costly. In 2020, 486,000 autos valued at over $500 million were stolen. About 28 percent of the inhabitants of federal prisons are there as a result of conviction of interstate auto theft under the Dyer Act. In California alone, auto thefts cost the criminal justice system approximately $60 million yearly.

The great majority of auto theft is for temporary use rather than resale, as evidenced by the fact that 88 percent of autos stolen in 2020 were recovered. In Los Angeles, 64 percent of stolen autos that were recovered were found within two days and about 80 percent within a week. Chicago reports that 71 percent of the recovered autos were found within four miles of the point of theft. The FBI estimates that 8 percent of stolen cars are taken for the purpose of stripping them for parts, 12 percent for resale, and 5 percent for use in another crime. Auto thefts are primarily juvenile acts. Although only 21 percent of all arrests for nontraffic offenses in 2020 were of individuals under 18 years of age, 63 percent of auto theft arrests were of persons under 18. Auto theft represents the start of many criminal careers; in an FBI sample of juvenile auto theft offenders, 41 percent had no prior arrest record.

41. In the above passage, the discussion of the reasons for auto theft does NOT include the percent of 41.____
   A. autos stolen by prior offenders
   B. recovered stolen autos found close to the point of theft
   C. stolen autos recovered within a week
   D. stolen autos which were recovered

42. Assuming the figures in the above passage remain constant, you may logically estimate the cost of auto thefts to the California criminal justice system over a five-year period beginning in 2020 to have been about _____ million. 42.____
   A. $200 B. $300 C. $440 D. $500

43. According to the above passage, the percent of stolen autos in Los Angeles which were not recovered within a week was _____ percent. 43.____
   A. 12 B. 20 C. 29 D. 36

44. According to the above passage, MOST auto thefts are committed by 44.____
   A. former inmates of federal prisons
   B. juveniles
   C. persons with a prior arrest record
   D. residents of large cities

45. According to the above passage, MOST autos are stolen for 45.____
   A. resale B. stripping of parts
   C. temporary use D. use in another crime

46. According to the above passage, the percent of persons arrested for auto theft who were under 18 46.____
    A. equals nearly the same percent of stolen autos which were recovered
    B. equals nearly two-thirds of the total number of persons arrested for nontraffic offenses
    C. is the same as the percent of persons arrested for nontraffic offenses who were under 18
    D. is three times the percent of persons arrested for nontraffic offenses who were under 18

47. An APPROPRIATE title for the above passage is 47.____
    A. How Criminal Careers Begin
    B. Recovery of Stolen Cars
    C. Some Statistics on Auto Theft
    D. The Costs of Auto Theft

48. Based on the above passage, the number of cars taken for use in another crime in 2020 was 48.____
    A. 24,300
    B. 38,880
    C. 48,600
    D. 58,320

Questions 49-55.

DIRECTIONS: Questions 49 through 55 are to be answered SOLELY on the basis of the following passage.

Burglar alarms are designed to detect intrusion automatically. Robbery alarms enable a victim of a robbery or an attack to signal for help. Such devices can be located in elevators, hallways, homes and apartments, businesses and factories, and subways, as well as on the street in high-crime areas. Alarms could deter some potential criminals from attacking targets so protected. If alarms were prevalent and not visible, then they might serve to suppress crime generally. In addition, of course, the alarms can summon the police when they are needed.

All alarms must perform three functions: sensing or initiation of the signal, transmission of the signal, and annunciation of the alarm. A burglar alarm needs a sensor to detect human presence or activity in an unoccupied enclosed area like a building or a room. A robbery victim would initiate the alarm by closing a foot or wall switch, or by triggering a portable transmitter which would send the alarm signal to a remote receiver. The signal can sound locally as a loud noise to frighten away a criminal, or it can be sent silently by wire to a central agency. A centralized annunciator requires either private lines from each alarmed point, or the transmission of some information on the location of the signal.

49. A conclusion which follows LOGICALLY from the above passage is that 49.____
    A. burglar alarms employ sensor devices; robbery alarms make use of initiation devices
    B. robbery alarms signal intrusion without the help of the victim; burglar alarms require the victim to trigger a switch
    C. robbery alarms sound locally; burglar alarms are transmitted to a central agency
    D. the mechanisms for a burglar alarm and a robbery alarm are alike

50. According to the above passage, alarms can be located 50.____
A. in a wide variety of settings
B. only in enclosed areas
C. at low cost in high-crime areas
D. only in places where potential criminal will be deterred

51. According to the above passage, which of the following is ESSENTIAL if a signal is to be received in a central office? 51.____
A. A foot or wall switch
B. A noise producing mechanism
C. A portable reception device
D. Information regarding the location of the source

52. According to the above passage, an alarm system can function WITHOUT a 52.____
A. centralized annunciating device B. device to stop the alarm
C. sensing or initiating device D. transmission device

53. According to the above passage, the purpose of robbery alarms is to 53.____
A. find out automatically whether a robbery has taken place
B. lower the crime rate in high-crime areas
C. make a loud noise to frighten away the criminal
D. provide a victim with the means to signal for help

54. According to the above passage, alarms might aid in lessening crime if they were 54.____
A. answered promptly by police B. completely automatic
C. easily accessible to victims D. hidden and widespread

55. Of the following, the BEST title for the above passage is 55.____
A. Detection of Crime By Alarms B. Lowering the Crime Rate
C. Suppression of Crime D. The Prevention of Robbery

KEY (CORRECT ANSWERS)

1.	C	11.	C	21.	D	31.	D	41.	A	51.	D
2.	C	12.	D	22.	B	32.	B	42.	B	52.	A
3.	B	13.	A	23.	C	33.	A	43.	B	53.	D
4.	B	14.	D	24.	A	34.	C	44.	B	54.	D
5.	B	15.	A	25.	B	35.	C	45.	C	55.	A
6.	D	16.	A	26.	C	36.	D	46.	D		
7.	C	17.	B	27.	D	37.	B	47.	C		
8.	B	18.	B	28.	A	38.	A	48.	A		
9.	C	19.	B	29.	B	39.	A	49.	A		
10.	D	20.	B	30.	D	40.	D	50.	A		

SCANNING MAPS

One section of the exam tests your ability to orient yourself within a given region on a map. Using the map accompanying questions 1 through 3; choose the best way of getting from one point to another.

The New Bridge is closed to traffic because it has a broken span.

MAP 1

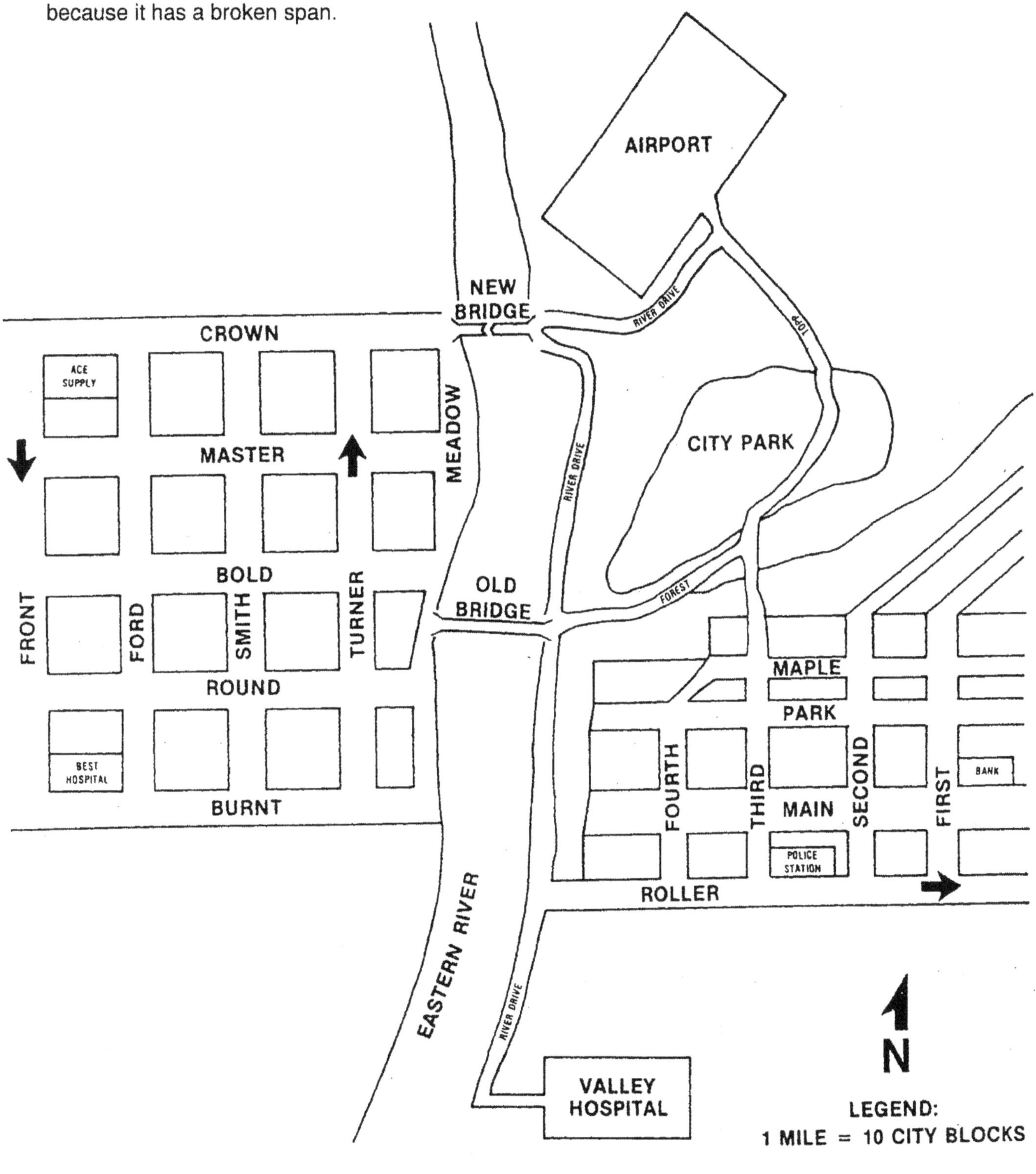

Arrows (⟶) indicate on-way traffic and direction of traffic. A street marked by an arrow is one way for the entire length of the street.

SAMPLE QUESTIONS

1. Officers in a patrol car which is at the Airport receive a call for assistance at Best Hospital. The shortest route without breaking the law is:
   A. Southwest on River Drive, right on Forest, cross Old Bridge, south on Meadow, and west on Burnt to hospital entrance.
   B. Southwest on River Drive, right on New Bridge, left on Meadow, west on Burnt to hospital entrance.
   C. Southwest on River Drive, right on Old Bridge, left on Turner, right on Burnt to hospital entrance.
   D. North on River Drive to Topp, through City Park to Forest, cross Old Bridge, left on Meadow, west on Burnt to hospital entrance.

2. After returning to the police station, the officers receive a call to pick up injured persons at an accident site (located on the east side of New Bridge) and return to Valley Hospital. The shortest route without breaking the law is:

   A. West on Roller, north on River Drive, left to accident scene at New Bridge, then north on River Drive to hospital entrance.
   B. North on Third, left on Forest, north on River Drive, left to accident scene at new Bridge, then south on River Drive to hospital entrance.
   C. East on Roller, left on First, west on Maple, north on Third, left on Forest, north on River Drive to accident scene at New Bridge, then south on River Drive to hospital entrance.
   D. North on Third, left on Forest, cross Old Bridge, north on Meadow to New Bridge, south on Meadow, east over Old Bridge, then south on River Drive to hospital entrance.

3. While at the Valley Hospital, the officers receive a call asking them to pick up materials at the Ace Supply and return them to the police station. The shortest route without breaking the law is:
   A. North on River Drive, cross New Bridge, west on Crown to Ace Supply, then south on Front, east on Burnt, north on Meadow, cross Old Bridge, east on Forest, south on Third to police station.
   B. North on River Drive, right on Roller to police station, then north on Third, left on Forest, cross Old Bridge, north on Meadow, west on Crown to Ace Supply.
   C. North on River Drive, cross Old Bridge, north on Meadow, west on Crown to Ace Supply, then east on Crown, south on Meadow, cross Old Bridge, east on Forest, south on Third to police station.
   D. North on River Drive, cross Old Bridge, south on Meadow, west on Burnt, north on Front to Ace Supply, then east on Crown, south on Meadow, cross Old Bridge, east on Forest, south on Third to police station.

KEY (CORRECT ANSWERS)

1. A
2. B
3. C

MAP READING

EXAMINATION SECTION
TEST 1

DIRECTIONS: Each question or incomplete statement is followed by several suggested answers or completions. Select the one that BEST answers the question or completes the statement. *PRINT THE LETTER OF THE CORRECT ANSWER IN THE SPACE AT THE RIGHT.*

Questions 1-3.

DIRECTIONS: Questions 1 through 3 are to be answered SOLELY on the basis of the map which appears on the next page. The flow of traffic is indicated by the arrow. If there is only one arrow shown, then traffic flows only in the direction indicated by the arrow. If there are two arrows shown, then traffic flows in both directions. You must follow the flow of traffic.

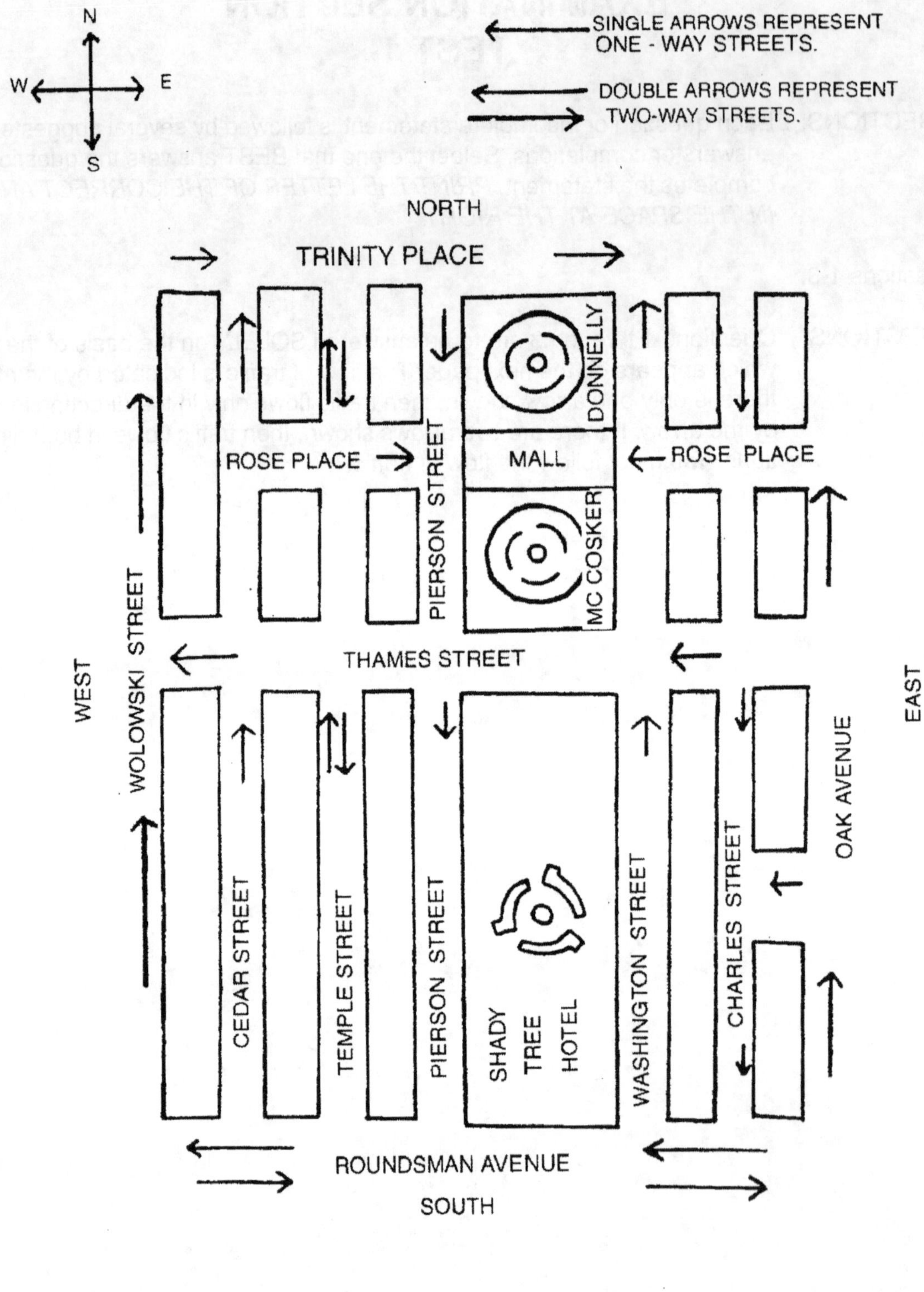
N
W
E
S
SINGLE ARROWS REPRESENT ONE - WAY STREETS.
DOUBLE ARROWS REPRESENT TWO-WAY STREETS.
NORTH
TRINITY PLACE
DONNELLY
ROSE PLACE
MALL
ROSE PLACE
PIERSON STREET
MC COSKER
WOLOWSKI STREET
THAMES STREET
WEST
EAST
OAK AVENUE
CHARLES STREET
CEDAR STREET
TEMPLE STREET
PIERSON STREET
SHADY TREE HOTEL
WASHINGTON STREET
ROUNDSMAN AVENUE
SOUTH

1. Police Officers Simms and O'Brien are located at Roundsman Avenue and Washington Street. The radio dispatcher has assigned them to investigate a motor vehicle accident at the corner of Pierson Street and Rose Place. 1.____
Which one of the following is the SHORTEST route for them to take in their patrol car, making sure to obey all traffic regulations?
Travel

   A. west on Roundsman Avenue, then north on Temple Street, then east on Thames Street, then north on Pierson Street to Rose Place
   B. east on Roundsman Avenue, then north on Oak Avenue, then west on Rose Place to Pierson Street
   C. west on Roundsman Avenue, then north on Temple Street, then east on Rose Place to Pierson Street
   D. east on Roundsman Avenue, then north on Oak Avenue, then west on Thames Street, then north on Temple Street, then east on Rose Place to Pierson Street

2. Police Officers Sears and Castro are located at Cedar Street and Roundsman Avenue. They are called to respond to the scene of a burglary at Rose Place and Charles Street. 2.____
Which one of the following is the SHORTEST route for them to take in their patrol car, making sure to obey all traffic regulations?
Travel

   A. east on Roundsman Avenue, then north on Oak Avenue, then west on Rose Place to Charles Street
   B. east on Roundsman Avenue, then north on Washington Street, then east on Rose Place to Charles Street
   C. west on Roundsman Avenue, then north on Wolowski Street, then east on Trinity Place, then south on Charles Street to Rose Place
   D. east on Roundsman Avenue, then north on Charles Street to Rose Place

3. Police Officer Glasser is in an unmarked car at the intersection of Rose Place and Temple Street when he begins to follow two robbery suspects. The suspects go south for two blocks, then turn left for two blocks, then make another left turn for one more block. The suspects realize they are being followed and make a left turn and travel two more blocks and then make a right turn. 3.____
In what direction are the suspects now headed?

   A. North   B. South   C. East   D. West

Questions 4-6.

DIRECTIONS: Questions 4 through 6 are to be answered SOLELY on the basis of the following map. The flow of traffic is indicated by the arrows. If there is only one arrow shown, then traffic flows only in the direction indicated by the arrow. If there are two arrows shown, then traffic flows in both directions. You must follow the flow of traffic.

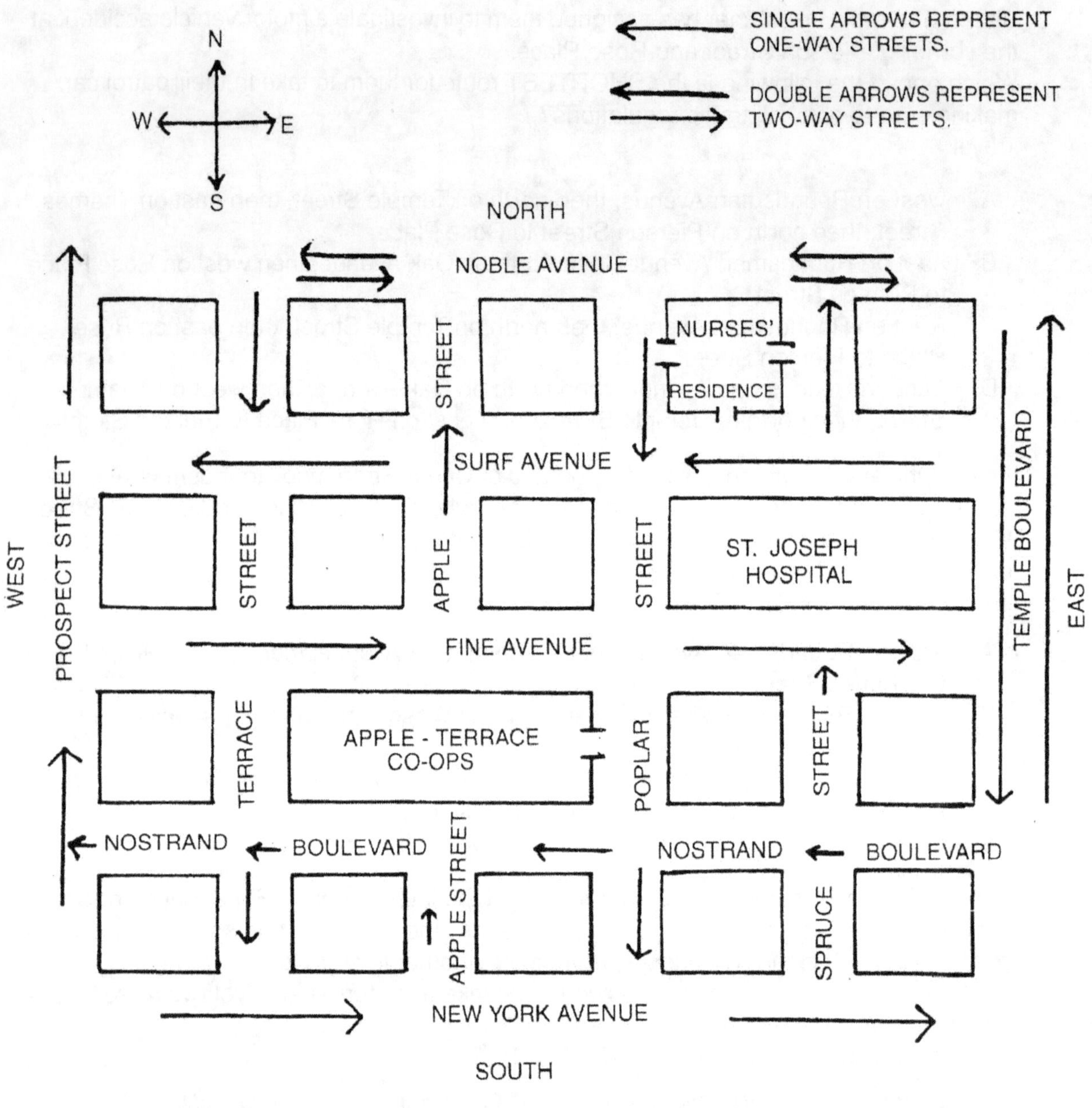

4. Police Officers Gannon and Vine are located at the intersection of Terrace Street and Surf Avenue when they receive a call from the radio dispatcher stating that they need to respond to an attempted murder at Spruce Street and Fine Avenue. Which one of the following is the SHORTEST route for them to take in their patrol car, making sure to obey all traffic regulations?
Travel ______ to Spruce Street. 4.______

A. west on Surf Avenue, then north on Prospect Street, then east on Noble Avenue, then south on Poplar Street, then east on Fine Avenue
B. east on Surf Avenue, then south on Poplar Street, then east on Fine Avenue
C. west on Surf Avenue, then south on Prospect Street, then east on Fine Avenue
D. south on Terrace Street, then east on Fine Avenue

5. Police Officers Sears and Ronald are at Nostrand Boulevard and Prospect Street. They receive a call assigning them to investigate a disruptive group of youths at Temple Boulevard and Surf Avenue. 5.____
Which one of the following is the SHORTEST route for them to take in their patrol car, making sure to obey all traffic regulations?
Travel

A. north on Prospect Street, then east on Surf Avenue to Temple Boulevard
B. north on Prospect Street, then east on Noble Avenue, then south on Temple Boulevard to Surf Avenue
C. north on Prospect Street, then east on Fine Avenue, then north on Temple Boulevard to Surf Avenue
D. south on Prospect Street, then east on New York Avenue, then north on Temple Boulevard to Surf Avenue

6. While on patrol at Prospect Street and New York Avenue, Police Officers Ross and Rock are called to a burglary in progress near the entrance to the Apple-Terrace Co-ops on Poplar Street midway between Fine Avenue and Nostrand Boulevard. 6.____
Which one of the following is the SHORTEST route for them to take in their patrol car, making sure to obey all traffic regulations?
Travel ______ Poplar Street.

A. east on New York Avenue, then north
B. north on Prospect Avenue, then east on Fine Avenue, then south
C. north on Prospect Street, then east on Surf Avenue, then south
D. east on New York Avenue, then north on Temple Boulevard, then west on Surf Avenue, then south

Questions 7-8.

DIRECTIONS: Questions 7 and 8 are to be answered SOLELY on the basis of the map which appears below. The flow of traffic is indicated by the arrows. If there is only one arrow shown, then traffic flows only in the direction indicated by the arrow. If there are two arrows shown, then traffic flows in both directions. You must follow the flow of traffic.

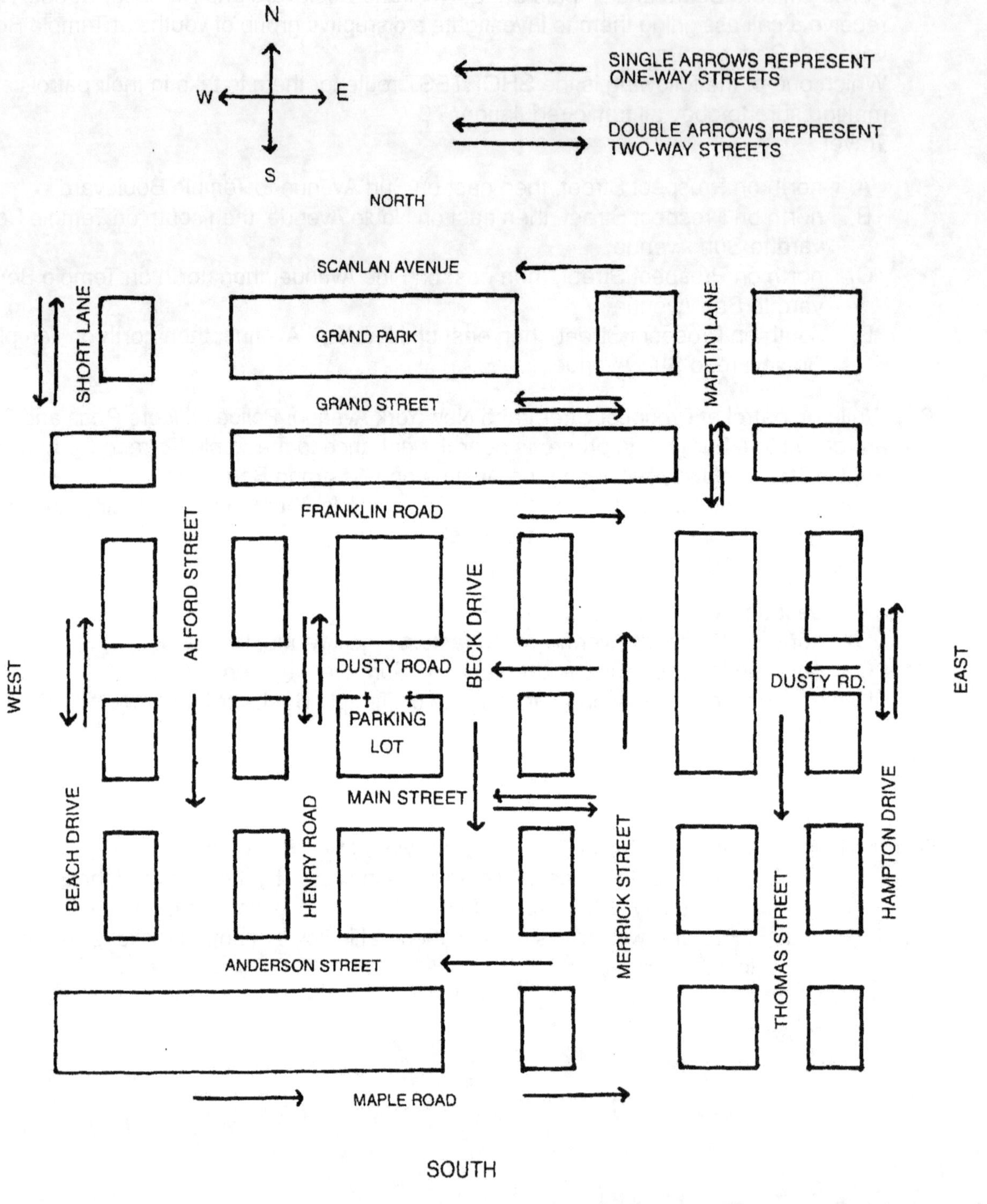

7. Police Officers Gold and Warren are at the intersection of Maple Road and Hampton Drive. The radio dispatcher has assigned them to investigate an attempted auto theft in the parking lot on Dusty Road. 7.___
Which one of the following is the SHORTEST route for the officers to take in their patrol car to get to the entrance of the parking lot on Dusty Road, making sure to obey all traffic regulations?
Travel ______ to the parking lot entrance.

A. north on Hampton Drive, then west on Dusty Road
B. west on Maple Road, then north on Beck Drive, then west on Dusty Road
C. north on Hampton Drive, then west on Anderson Street, then north on Merrick Street, then west on Dusty Road
D. west on Maple Road, then north on Merrick Street, then west on Dusty Road

8. Police Officer Gladden is in a patrol car at the intersection of Beach Drive and Anderson Street when he spots a suspicious car. Police Officer Gladden calls the radio dispatcher to determine if the vehicle was stolen. Police Officer Gladden then follows the vehicle north on Beach Drive for three blocks, then turns right and proceeds for one block and makes another right. He then follows the vehicle for two blocks, and then they both make a left turn and continue driving. Police Officer Gladden now receives a call from the dispatcher stating the car was reported stolen and signals for the vehicle to pull to the side of the road. 8.____
In what direction was Police Officer Gladden heading at the time he signaled for the other car to pull over?

A. North B. East C. South D. West

Questions 9-10.

DIRECTIONS: Questions 9 and 10 are to be answered SOLELY on the basis of the map which appears on the following page. The flow of traffic is indicated by the arrows. If there is only one arrow shown, then traffic flows only in the direction indicated by the arrow. If there are two arrows shown, then traffic flows in both directions. You must follow the flow of traffic.

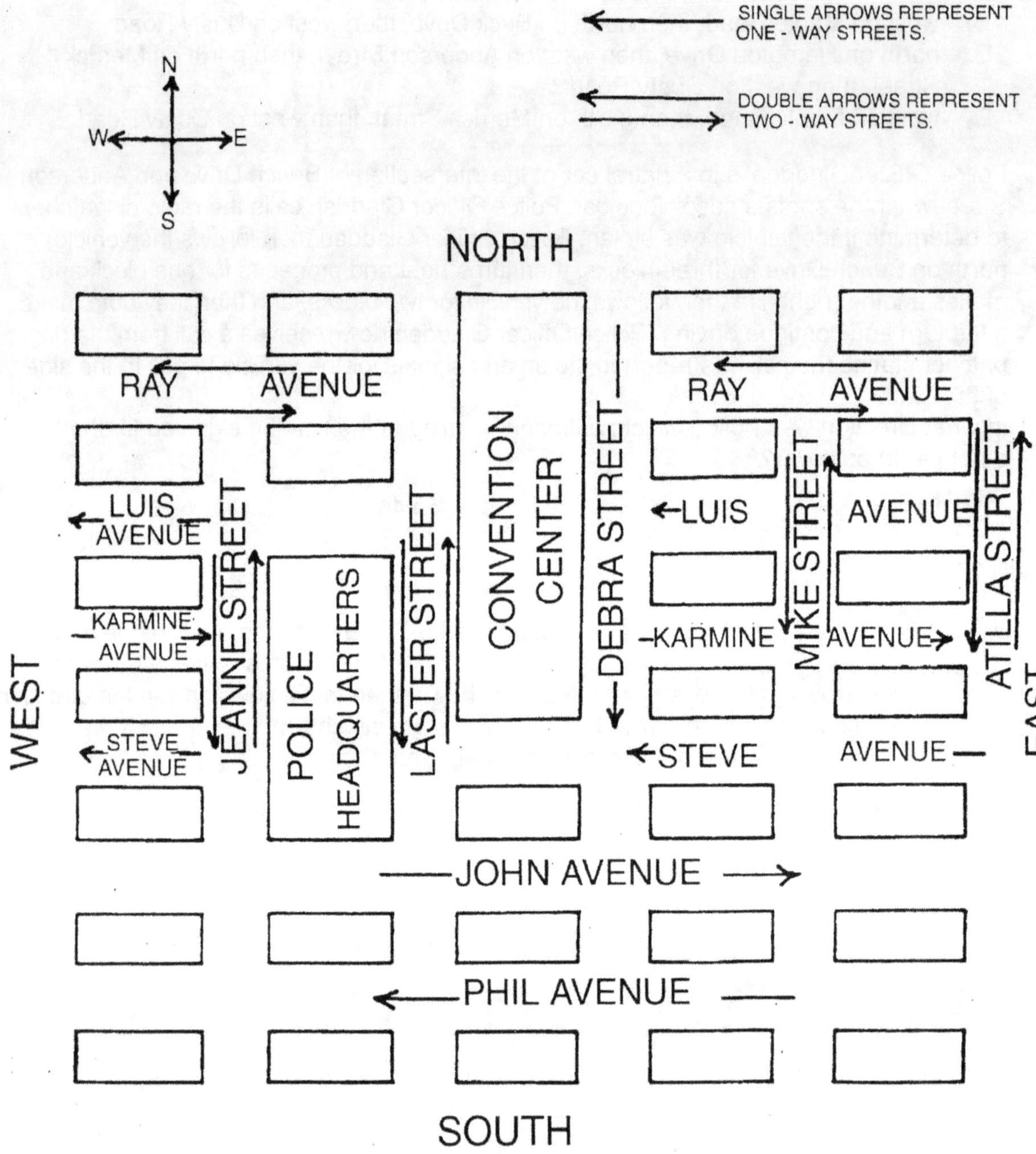

9. While in a patrol car located at Ray Avenue and Atilla Street, Police Officer Ashley receives a call from the dispatcher to respond to an assault at Jeanne Street and Karmine Avenue. 9.____
Which one of the following is the SHORTEST route for Officer Ashley to follow in his patrol car, making sure to obey all traffic regulations?
Travel

A. south on Atilla Street, west on Luis Avenue, south on Debra Street, west on Steve Avenue, north on Lester Street, west on Luis Avenue, then one block south on Jeanne Street
B. south on Atilla Street, then four blocks west on Phil Avenue, then north on Jeanne Street to Karmine Avenue

C. west on Ray Avenue to Debra Street, then five blocks south to Phil Avenue, then west to Jeanne Street, then three blocks north to Karmine Avenue
D. south on Atilla Street, then four blocks west on John Avenue, then north on Jeanne Street to Karmine Avenue

10. After taking a complaint report from the assault victim, Officer Ashley receives a call from the dispatcher to respond to an auto larceny in progress at the corner of Debra Street and Luis Avenue. 10.____
Which one of the following is the SHORTEST route for Officer Ashley to follow in his patrol car, making sure to obey all traffic regulations?
Travel

A. south on Jeanne Street to John Avenue, then east three blocks on John Avenue, then north on Mike Street to Luis Avenue, then west to Debra Street
B. south on Jeanne Street to John Avenue, then east two blocks on John Avenue, then north on Debra Street to Luis Avenue
C. north on Jeanne Street two blocks, then east on Ray Avenue for one block, then south on Lester Street to Steve Avenue, then one block east on Steve Avenue, then north on Debra Street to Luis Avenue
D. south on Jeanne Street to John Avenue, then east on John Avenue to Atilla Street, then north three blocks to Luis Avenue, then west to Debra Street

Questions 11-13.

DIRECTIONS: Questions 11 through 13 are to be answered SOLELY on the basis of the following map. The flow of traffic is indicated by the arrows. You must follow the flow of traffic.

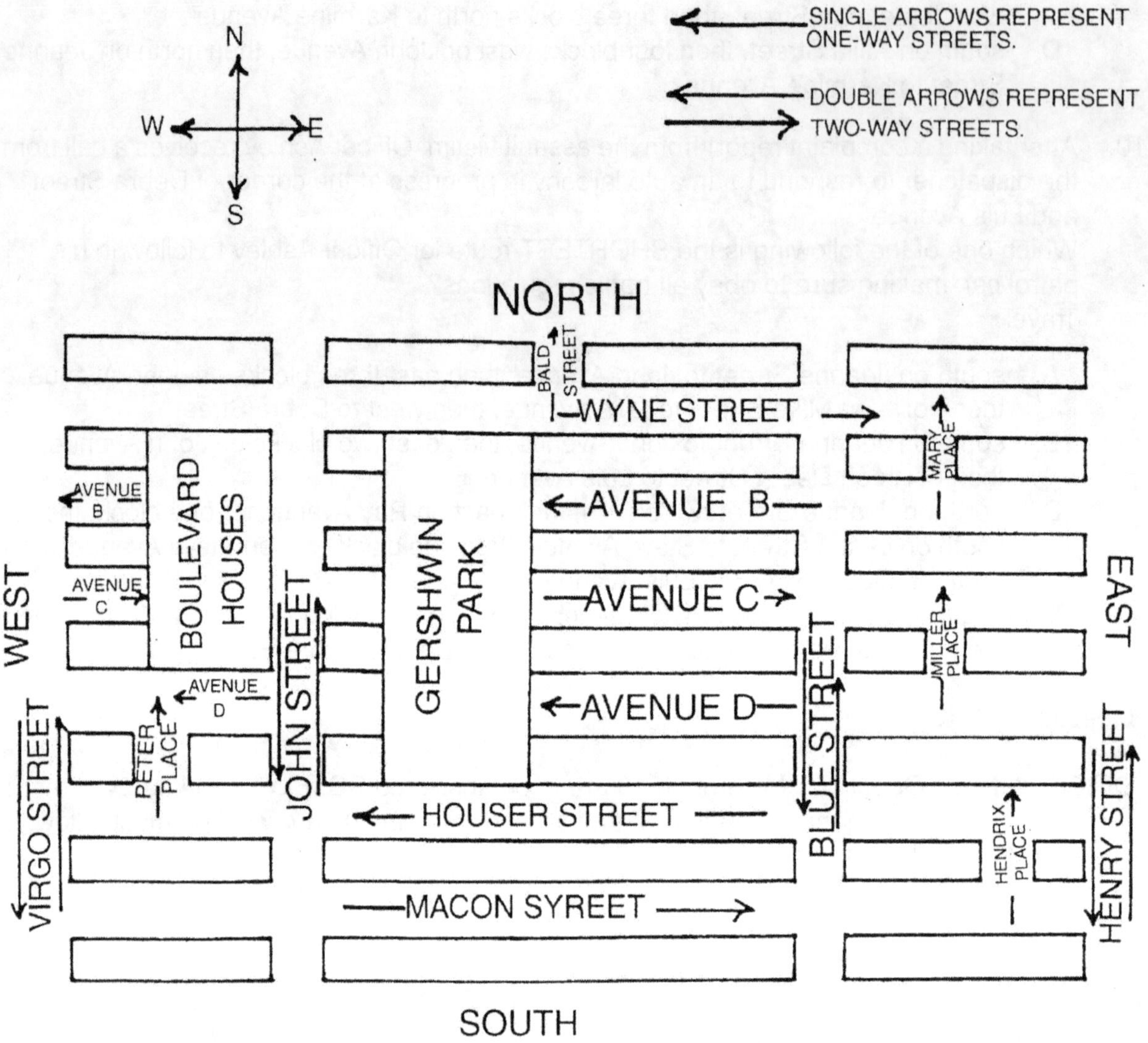

11. Police Officers Ranking and Fish are located at Wyne Street and John Street. The radio dispatcher has assigned them to investigate a motor vehicle accident at the corner of Henry Street and Houser Street. 11.____
Which one of the following is the SHORTEST route for them to take in their patrol car, making sure to obey all traffic regulations?
Travel

A. four blocks south on John Street, then three blocks east on Houser Street to Henry Street
B. two blocks east on Wyne Street, then two blocks south on Blue Street, then two blocks east on Avenue C, then two blocks south on Henry Street
C. two blocks east on Wyne Street, then five blocks south on Blue Street, then two blocks east on Macon Street, then one block north on Henry Street
D. five blocks south on John Street, then three blocks east on Macon Street, then one block north to Houser Street

12. Police Officers Rizzo and Latimer are located at Avenue B and Virgo Street. They respond to the scene of a robbery at Miller Place and Avenue D. Which one of the following is the SHORTEST route for them to take in their patrol car, making sure to obey all traffic regulations? Travel ______ to Miller Place. 12.____

A. one block north on Virgo Street, then four blocks east on Wyne Street, then three blocks south on Henry Street, then one block west on Avenue D
B. four blocks south on Virgo Street, then two blocks east on Macon Street, then two blocks north on Blue Street, then one block east on Avenue D
C. three blocks south on Virgo Street, then east on Houser Street to Henry Street, then one block north on Henry Street, then one block west on Avenue D
D. four blocks south on Virgo Street, then four blocks east to Henry Street, then north to Avenue D, then one block west

13. Police Officer Bendix is in an unmarked patrol car at the intersection of John Street and Macon Street when he begins to follow a robbery suspect. The suspect goes one block east, turns left, travels for three blocks, and then turns right. He drives for two blocks and then makes a right turn. In the middle of the block, the suspect realizes he is being followed and makes a u-turn. In what direction is the suspect now headed? 13.____

A. North B. South C. East D. West

Questions 14-15.

DIRECTIONS: Questions 14 and 15 are to be answered SOLELY on the basis of the following map. The flow of traffic is indicated by the arrows. If there is only one arrow shown, then traffic flows only in the direction indicated by the arrow. If there are two arrows shown, then traffic flows in both directions. You must follow the flow of traffic.

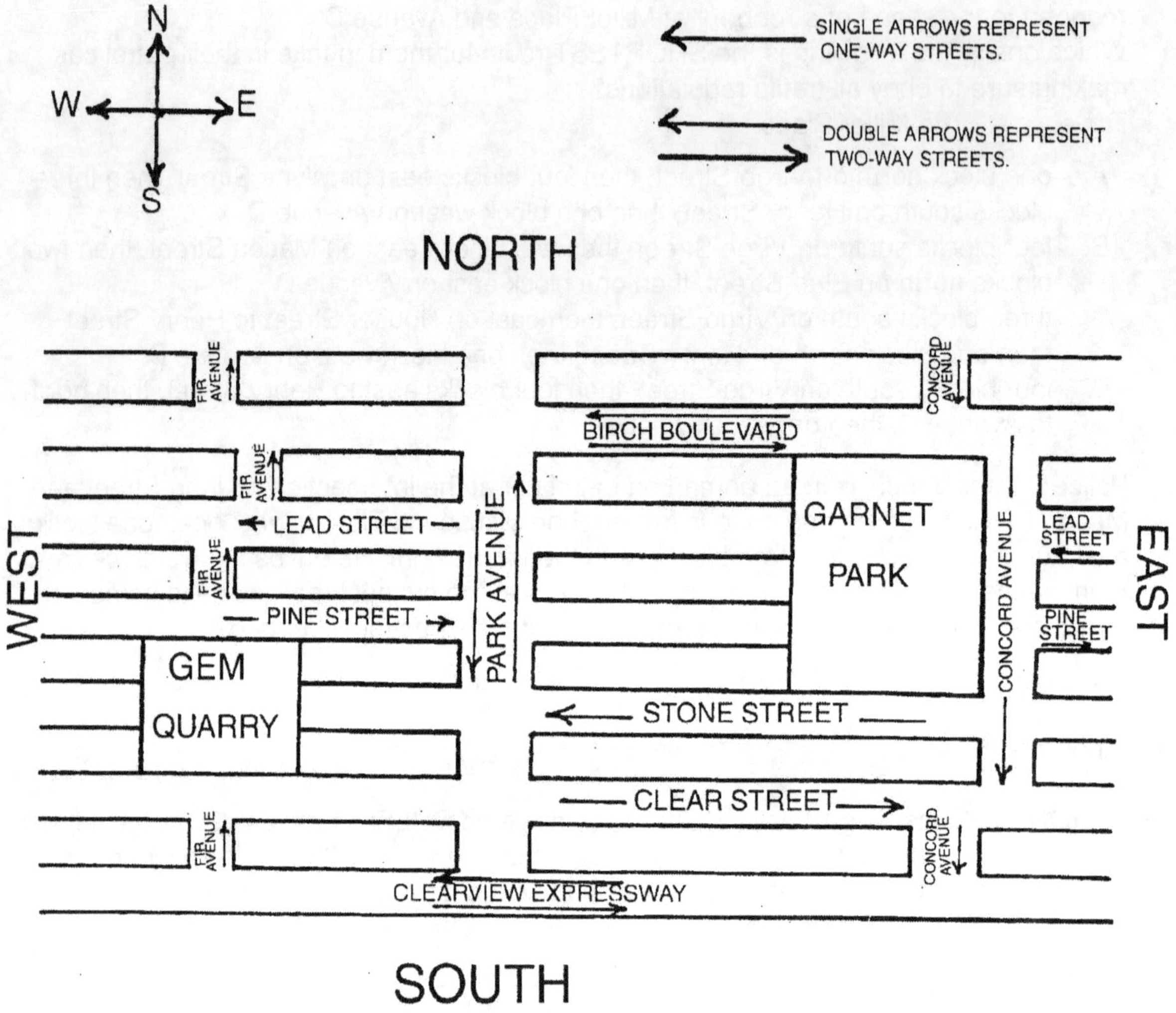

14. You are located at Fir Avenue and Birch Boulevard and receive a request to respond to a disturbance at Fir Avenue and Clear Street. 14.____
Which one of the following is the MOST direct route for you to take in your patrol car, making sure to obey all traffic regulations?
Travel

A. one block east on Birch Boulevard, then four blocks south on Park Avenue, then one block east on Clear Street
B. two blocks east on Birch Boulevard, then three blocks south on Concord Avenue, then two blocks west on Stone Street, then one block south on Park Avenue, then one block west on Clear Street
C. one block east on Birch Boulevard, then five blocks south on Park Avenue, then one block west on the Clearview Expressway, then one block north on Fir Avenue
D. two blocks south on Fir Avenue, then one block east on Pine Street, then three blocks south on Park Avenue, then one block east on the Clearview Expressway, then one block north on Fir Avenue

15. You are located at the Clearview Expressway and Concord Avenue and receive a call to respond to a crime in progress at Concord Avenue and Pine Street. Which one of the following is the MOST direct route for you to take in your patrol car, making sure to obey all traffic regulations? 15.____
Travel

A. two blocks west on the Clearview Expressway, then one block north on Fir Avenue, then one block east on Clear Street, then four blocks north on Park Avenue, then one block east on Birch Boulevard, then two blocks south on Concord Avenue
B. one block north on Concord Avenue, then one block west on Clear Street, then one block north on Park Avenue, then one block east on Stone Street, then one block north on Concord Avenue
C. one block west on the Clearview Expressway, then four blocks north on Park Avenue, then one block west on Lead Street, then one block south on Fir Avenue
D. one block west on the Clearview Expressway, then five blocks north on Park Avenue, then one block east on Birch Boulevard, then two blocks south on Concord Avenue

Questions 16-20.

DIRECTIONS: Questions 16 through 20 are to be answered SOLELY on the basis of the following map. The flow of traffic is indicated by the arrows. You must follow the flow of traffic.

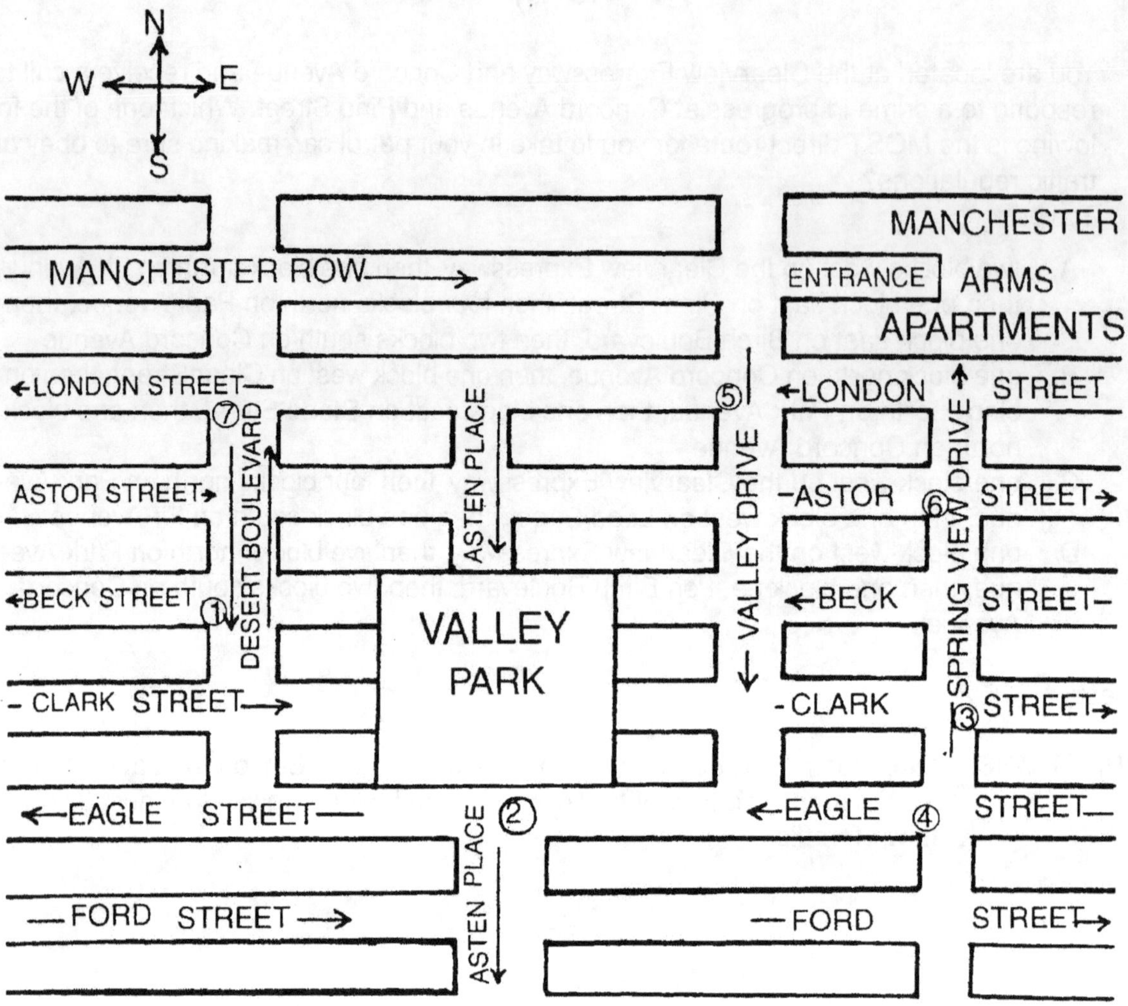

16. If you are located at Point 7 and travel south for one block, then turn east and travel two blocks, then turn south and travel two blocks, then turn east and travel one block, you will be CLOSEST to Point 16.____

A. 2 B. 3 C. 4 D. 6

17. If you are located at Point 3 and travel north for one block, and then turn west and travel one block, and then turn south and travel two blocks, and then turn west and travel one block, you will be CLOSEST to Point 17.____

A. 1 B. 2 C. 4 D. 6

18. You are located at Astor Street and Spring View Drive. You receive a call of a crime in progress at the intersection of Beck Street and Desert Boulevard. 18.____
Which one of the following is the MOST direct route for you to take in your patrol car, making sure to obey all traffic regulations?
Travel

A. one block north on Spring View Drive, then three blocks west on London Street, then two blocks south on Desert Boulevard
B. three blocks west on Astor Street, then one block south on Desert Boulevard

C. one block south on Spring View Drive, then three blocks west on Beck Street
D. three blocks south on Spring View Drive, then three blocks west on Eagle Street, then two blocks north on Desert Boulevard

19. You are located on Clark Street and Desert Boulevard and must respond to a disturbance at Clark Street and Spring View Drive. 19.____
Which one of the following is the MOST direct route for you to take in your patrol car, making sure to obey all traffic regulations?
Travel

A. two blocks north on Desert Boulevard, then three blocks east on Astor Street, then two blocks south on Spring View Drive
B. one block south on Desert Boulevard, then three blocks east on Eagle Street, then one block north on Spring View Drive
C. two blocks north on Desert Boulevard, then two blocks east on Astor Street, then three blocks south on Valley Drive, then one block east on Eagle Street, then one block north on Spring View Drive
D. two blocks north on Desert Boulevard, then two blocks east on Astor Street, then two blocks south on Valley Drive, then one block east on Clark Street

20. You are located at Valley Drive and Beck Street and receive a call to respond to the corner of Asten Place and Astor Street. 20.____
Which one of the following is the MOST direct route for you to take in your patrol car, making sure to obey all traffic regulations?
Travel ______ on Astor Street.

A. one block north on Valley Drive, then one block west
B. two blocks south on Valley Drive, then one block east on Eagle Street, then three blocks north on Spring View Drive, then two blocks west
C. two blocks south on Valley Drive, then two blocks west on Eagle Street, then three blocks north on Desert Boulevard, then one block east
D. one block south on Valley Drive, then one block east on Clark Street, then two blocks north on Spring View Drive, then two blocks west

KEY (CORRECT ANSWERS)

1.	C	11.	B
2.	A	12.	A
3.	A	13.	A
4.	D	14.	C
5.	C	15.	D
6.	B	16.	B
7.	C	17.	B
8.	B	18.	A
9.	A	19.	D
10.	A	20.	C

READING COMPREHENSION
UNDERSTANDING AND INTERPRETING WRITTEN MATERIAL

EXAMINATION SECTION

TEST 1

DIRECTIONS: Each question or incomplete statement is followed by several suggested answers or completions. Select the one that BEST answers the question or completes the statement. *PRINT THE LETTER OF THE CORRECT ANSWER IN THE SPACE AT THE RIGHT.*

Questions 1-5.

DIRECTIONS: Questions 1 through 5 are to be answered SOLELY on the basis of the following passage.

Stopping, standing, and parking of motor vehicles is regulated by law to keep the public highways open for a smooth flow of traffic, and to keep stopped vehicles from blocking intersections, driveways, signs, fire hydrants, and other areas that must be kept clear. These established regulations apply in all situations, unless otherwise indicated by signs. Other local restrictions are posted in the areas to which they apply. Three examples of these other types of restrictions, which may apply singly or in combination with one another, are:

NO STOPPING: This means that a driver may not stop a vehicle for any purpose except when necessary to avoid interference with other vehicles, or in compliance with directions of a police officer or signal.

NO STANDING: This means that a driver may stop a vehicle only temporarily to actually receive or discharge passengers.

NO PARKING: This means that a driver may stop a vehicle only temporarily to actually load or unload merchandise or passengers. When stopped, it is advisable to turn on warning flashers if equipped with them. However, one should never use a directional signal for this purpose, because it may confuse the other drivers. Some NO PARKING signs prohibit parking between certain hours on certain days. For example, the sign may read NO PARKING 8 A.M. TO 11 A.M. MONDAY, WEDNESDAY, FRIDAY. These signs are usually utilized on streets where cleaning operations take place on alternate days.

1. The parking regulation that applies to fire hydrants is an example of _____ regulations. 1.____
   A. local B. established C. posted D. temporary

2. When stopped in a NO PARKING zone, it is ADVISABLE to 2.____
   A. turn on the right directional signal to indicate to other drivers that you will remain stopped
   B. turn on the left directional signal to indicate to other drivers that you may be leaving the curb after a period of time

C. turn on the warning flashers if your car is equipped with them
D. put the vehicle in reverse so that the backup lights will be on to warn approaching cars that you have temporarily stopped

3. You may stop a vehicle temporarily to discharge passengers in an area under the restriction of a _____ zone. 3.____
A. NO STOPPING – NO STANDING
B. NO STANDING – NO PARKING
C. NO PARKING – NO STOPPING
D. NO STOPPING – NO STANDING – NO PARKING

4. A sign reads NO PARKING 8 A.M. TO 11 A.M., MONDAY, WEDNESDAY, FRIDAY. 4.____
Based on this sign, a parking enforcement agent would issue a summons to a car that is parked on a _____ at _____ A.M.
A. Tuesday; 9:30
B. Wednesday; 12:00
C. Friday; 10:30
D. Saturday; 8:00

5. NO PARKING signs prohibiting parking between certain hours, on certain days, are USUALLY utilized on streets where 5.____
A. vehicles frequently take on and discharge passengers
B. cleaning operations take place on alternate days
C. NO STOPPING signs have been ignored
D. commercial vehicles take on and unload merchandise

Questions 6-15.

DIRECTIONS: Questions 6 through 15 are to be answered SOLELY on the basis of the following passage.

Parking Enforcement Agents in Iron City work three shifts. The first shift is from 10 A.M. to 6 P.M. The second shift is from 6 P.M. to 2 A.M. The third shift is from 2 A.M. to 10 A.M. Each shift at the Central Office employs three people who patrol the surrounding area. Parking Enforcement Agents have one hour off per shift for lunch.

Starting on Tuesday, Agents Fred Black, Mary Evans, and Thomas Hart worked the first shift. Harold Wilson and Mary Wood worked the second shift. The third agent for the second shift was ill. Thomas Hart worked the second shift in addition to his regular first shift, and thus earned overtime pay. Mike Brown, Anne Hill, and Jeff Smith worked the third shift.

On his first shift, Agent Thomas Hart wrote 11 summonses for meter violations, 15 summonses for double parking, and 13 summonses for parking in a no-standing zone. On his second shift, Thomas Hart wrote 21 summonses for double parking, 13 summonses for meter violations, and 15 summonses for parking in a no-standing zone.

6. On Tuesday, Agent Mary Wood was on duty from 6.____
A. 6 A.M. to 2 P.M.
B. 10 A.M. to 6 P.M.
C. 2 A.M. to 6 P.M.
D. 6 P.M. to 2 A.M.

7. How many Parking Enforcement Agents normally work from 6 P.M. to 2 A.M.? 7.____
   A. One B. Two C. Three D. Four

8. The number of Parking Enforcement Agents who ACTUALLY worked the second shift on Tuesday was 8.____
   A. one B. two C. three D. four

9. Among the three successive shifts which started on Tuesday, the total number of DIFFERENT Parking Enforcement Agents who actually reported for duty was 9.____
   A. 7 B. 8 C. 9 D. 10

10. The total number of summonses Agent Hart wrote during the FIRST shift he worked was 10.____
    A. 11 B. 13 C. 39 D. 49

11. Agent Hill was scheduled to finish her shift at 11.____
    A. 10 A.M. B. 6 P.M. C. 10 P.M. D. 2 A.M.

12. Parking Enforcement Agents have one hour off per shift. The TOTAL hours actually worked by Agent Evans on Tuesday was _____ hours. 12.____
    A. 8 B. 7½ C. 7 D. 6½

13. The TOTAL number of summonses Agent Hart wrote for meter violations was 13.____
    A. 15 B. 24 C. 26 D. 34

14. During both his shifts, Agent Hart wrote the MOST summonses for 14.____
    A. meter violations
    B. standing in a no-parking zone
    C. double parking
    D. parking in a no-standing zone

15. The TOTAL number of summonses Agent Hart wrote during his two shifts was 15.____
    A. 28 B. 48 C. 68 D. 88

Questions 16-22.

DIRECTIONS: Questions 16 through 22 are to be answered SOLELY on the basis of the following passage.

The parking meter was designed 30 years ago primarily as a mechanism to assist in reducing overtime parking at the curb, to increase parking turnover, and to facilitate enforcement of parking regulations. That the meter has accomplished these basic functions is attested to by its use in an increasing number of cities.

A recent survey of cities in the United States indicates that overtime parking was reduced 75% or more in 47% of the cities surveyed, and to a lesser degree in 43% of the cities surveyed, making a total of 90% of the cities surveyed where the parking meter was found to be effective in reducing overtime parking at the curb.

A side effect of the reduction in overtime parking is the increase in parking turnover. Approximately 89% of the places surveyed found meters useful in this respect. Meters also encourage even spacing of cars at the curb. Unmetered curb parking is often so irregular that it wastes space or makes parking and departure difficult.

The effectiveness of parking meters, in the final analysis, rests upon the enforcement of regulations by squads of enforcement agents who will diligently patrol the metered area. The task of checking parking time is made easier with meters, since violations can be checked from a moving vehicle or by visual sightings of an agent on foot patrol, and the laborious process of chalking tires is greatly reduced. It is reported that, after meters have been installed, it takes on the average only 25% of the time formerly required to patrol the same area.

The fact that a parker activates a mechanism that immediately begins to count time, that will indicate exactly when the parking time has expired, and that will advertise such fact by showing a red flag, tends to make a parker more conscious of his parking responsibilities than the hit and miss system of possible detection by a patrolman.

16. According to the above passage, when the parking meter was introduced, one of its major purposes was NOT to 16.____
   A. cut down overtime curb parking
   B. make curb parking available to more parkers
   C. bring in revenue from parking fees
   D. make it easier to enforce parking regulations

17. In the cities surveyed, how effective was the installation of parking meters in cutting down overtime parking? 17.____
   A. It was effective to some degree in all of the cities surveyed.
   B. It was ineffective in only one out of every ten cities surveyed.
   C. It reduced overtime parking at least 75% in most cities surveyed.
   D. There was only a small reduction in overtime parking in 43% of the cities surveyed.

18. When overtime parking is reduced by the installation of parking meters, an accompanying result is 18.____
   A. an increase in the amount of parking space
   B. the use of the available parking spaces by more cars
   C. the faster movement of traffic
   D. a decrease in the number of squads required to enforce traffic regulations

19. According to the above passage, on streets which have parking meters, as compared with streets which are unmetered, 19.____
   A. there is less waste of parking space
   B. parking is more difficult
   C. parking time limits are irregular
   D. drivers waste more time looking for an empty parking space

20. According to the above passage, the use of parking meters will NOT be effective unless 20.____
   A. parking areas are patrolled in automobiles
   B. it is combined with the chalking of tires
   C. the public cooperates
   D. there is strict enforcement of parking regulations

21. According to the above passage, one reason why there is greater compliance with parking regulations when parking time is regulated by meters rather than by a foot patrolman chalking tires is that 21.____
   A. overtime parking becomes glaringly evident to everyone
   B. the parker is himself responsible for operating the timing mechanism
   C. there is no personal relationship between parker and enforcing officer
   D. the timing of elapsed parking time is accurate

22. In the last paragraph of the above passage, the words *a parker activates a mechanism* refers to the fact that a motorist 22.____
   A. starts the timing device of the meter working
   B. parks his car
   C. checks whether the meter is working
   D. starts the engine of his car

Questions 23-25.

DIRECTIONS: Questions 6 through 15 are to be answered SOLELY on the basis of the information given in the following passage.

When markings upon the curb or the pavement of a street designate parking space, no person shall stand or park a vehicle in such designated parking space so that any part of such vehicle occupies more than one such space or protrudes beyond the markings designating such a space, except that a vehicle which is a size too large to be parked within a single designated parking space shall be parked with the front bumper at the front of the space with the rear of the vehicle extending as little as possible into the adjoining space to the rear, or vice-versa.

23. The regulation quoted above applies to parking at any 23.____
   A. curb or pavement
   B. metered spaces
   C. street where parking is permitted
   D. parking spaces with marked boundaries

24. The regulation quoted above prohibits the occupying of more than one indicated parking space by 24.____
   A. any vehicle
   B. large vehicles
   C. small vehicles
   D. vehicles in spaces partially occupied

25. In the regulation quoted above, the term *vice-versa* refers to a vehicle of a size too large parked with 25.____
    A. front bumper flush with front of parking space it occupies
    B. front of vehicle extending into front of parking space
    C. rear bumper flush with rear of parking space it occupies
    D. rear of vehicle protruding into adjoining parking space

KEY (CORRECT ANSWERS)

1.	B	11.	A
2.	C	12.	C
3.	B	13.	B
4.	C	14.	C
5.	B	15.	D
6.	D	16.	C
7.	C	17.	B
8.	C	18.	B
9.	B	19.	A
10.	C	20.	D

21.	A
22.	A
23.	D
24.	C
25.	C

TEST 2

DIRECTIONS: Each question or incomplete statement is followed by several suggested answers or completions. Select the one that BEST answers the question or completes the statement. *PRINT THE LETTER OF THE CORRECT ANSWER IN THE SPACE AT THE RIGHT.*

Questions 1-5.

DIRECTIONS: Questions 1 through 5 are to be answered SOLELY on the basis of the following bulletin on SCHOOL ELIGIBILITY CARDS.

SCHOOL ELIGIBILITY CARDS

All bus operators are responsible for the proper use of School Eligibility Cards for reduced fares on their buses. These cards are issued to elementary and high school students. Such cards are good for the entire year from September 13 to June 28, and are issued subject to the following conditions:

A. The card is to be used by the student whose name appears on the face of the card, and only on days when school is in session. If offered by any other person, it will be taken away by the bus operator, and full fare will be collected from the person presenting the card.
B. The card will allow the student to ride on the particular bus indicated on the face of the card for a fare of fifty cents between 6 A.M. and 7 P.M. The fare of 50 cents must be deposited in the fare box by the student after the card is shown to the bus operator.
C. The student, after paying the 50 cent fare, is entitled to the same transfer privileges as other passengers.
D. The card will be taken away if altered or misused, and the student will not be given a new card for a period of five school months.
E. The card is not good unless all entries on the card are made by the teacher and the card is signed by the teacher.

1. If a student's School Eligibility Card is taken away by a bus operator because of misuse, the student will 1.____
   A. never be issued a new card because of this misuse
   B. not be issued a new card until he pays for the old one
   C. be eligible for a new card after five school months
   D. be eligible for a new card if he gets a note from his teacher

2. A bus operator should take away a School Eligibility Card if it is presented 2.____
   A. at 9 A.M. before school opens
   B. at 3 P.M. after school opens
   C. by a college student
   D. more than twice a day

3. A bus operator should permit a student to ride at reduced fare if he presents his School Eligibility Card at 3.____
   A. 8:00 A.M. on Sunday
   B. 8 A.M. on Monday
   C. 8:00 A.M. on Saturday
   D. 8:00 P.M. on Wednesday

4. If a student presents a School Eligibility Card, pays a 50 cent fare, and asks for a transfer, the bus operator should 4.____
   A. tell the student that during school hours he may not get a transfer
   B. tell him to use his School Eligibility Card instead
   C. give him a transfer if other passengers can get them free
   D. tell him he must pay the full dollar fare to get one

5. According to the above bulletin, School Eligibility Cards are NOT good on 5.____
   A. September 15
   B. October 26
   C. February 23
   D. June 30

Questions 6-12.

DIRECTIONS: Questions 6 through 12 are to be answered SOLELY on the basis of the following passage on the EXTRACT OF RULES FOR SYSTEM PICK FOR BUS OPERATORS.

EXTRACT OF RULES FOR SYSTEM PICK FOR BUS OPERATORS

Operators picking up an early run (one ending before 9:00 P.M., including all time allowances) on weekdays must pick an early run on Saturday and Sunday.

No operator will be allowed to pick on the extra list unless he desires to transfer to a depot where all runs, tricks, etc. have been picked.

After an operator finishes picking and the monitor has entered the operator's name for the run on the picking board, no change of run will be permitted. Erasures and other signs of mutilation will not be permitted on the picking board.

It is planned to permit about 100 operators in the picking room at one time, but the time allowed for any one person to pick will not exceed five minutes. If for any reason you cannot attend, you may submit a preference slip or be represented by proxy.

An operator inactive because of sickness, injury, etc. for sixty days prior to his pick assignment must present a certificate from a doctor stating he may return to duty not later than two weeks after date of pick.

Your cooperation is requested. Please be on hand to pick at your designated time, and leave picking room promptly when you have finished picking.

6. The rules apply to a pick of 6.____
   A. Saturday and Sunday
   B. depot extra
   C. weekday
   D. system

7. An operator picking an early run on weekdays 7.____
   A. cannot be off on Saturdays or Sundays
   B. must submit a preference slip
   C. will be assigned to the extra list on other days
   D. must pick an early run on Saturday and Sunday

8. According to the rules, an operator 8.____
   A. will be in the picking room alone while designating his choice
   B. must wait in the picking room after making his choice until all runs have been chosen
   C. is informed that he may pick his run at any time he wishes to on pick day
   D. may have someone else pick for him if he cannot be present on the day of the pick

9. In order to pick on the extra list, an operator MUST 9.____
   A. present a doctor's certificate
   B. have been inactive for sixty days
   C. appear at the picking room in person
   D. be willing to transfer to a terminal where all the runs have been picked

10. Once a bus operator picks a run and his name has been entered by the monitor, he 10.____
   A. must accept the run picked as no changes will be permitted
   B. can change his mind if the choice was made by proxy
   C. may ask the monitor to erase his pick if the next man has not yet picked
   D. can swap runs with another operator but only after sixty days

11. An operator making his pick after having been out sick for three months must 11.____
   A. pick on the extra list
   B. present a doctor's certificate to the monitor
   C. wait two weeks before returning to duty
   D. pick an early run or trick

12. The rules state that 12.____
   A. only 100 operators can pick in any one day
   B. cooperation is demanded, and a penalty will be imposed on any operator who is uncooperative
   C. a preference slip must be signed by the monitor
   D. an operator must make his pick within 5 minutes time

Questions 13-20.

DIRECTIONS: Questions 13 through 20 are to be answered SOLELY on the basis of the following passage on LOST PROPERTY.

LOST PROPERTY

When a passenger turns over a piece of lost property to a porter, or when a porter finds a lost article, he shall turn it in to the most convenient office equipped with a Lost Property bag and shall obtain a receipt therefor from the employee responsible for handling lost property. The responsible employee must forward articles of great value, such as expensive jewelry or large sums of money, to the Lost Property Office by special messenger as soon as possible and notify the Desk Trainmaster. The responsible employee must turn over all firearms to the Transit Police, take a proper receipt, and notify the Lost Property Office as soon as possible.

Perishable property, such as food products not in cans or boxes and requiring refrigeration, should be sold at the terminal by the terminal supervisor after holding for 8 hours, and the money forwarded to the Administrative Office; if the property is not sold, it should be destroyed and a record made on the lost property form.

13. A porter MUST turn over a lost umbrella at the _____ office. 13.____
    A. desk trainmaster's
    B. lost property
    C. transit police
    D. most convenient

14. A porter who finds a pistol on a station should take it to the _____ office. 14.____
    A. transit police
    B. lost property
    C. administrative
    D. most convenient

15. The Lost Property Office is mentioned 15.____
    A. once
    B. twice
    C. three times
    D. four times

16. If a porter finds a carton of canned peas, he should 16.____
    A. sell it
    B. destroy it
    C. keep it
    D. turn it in

17. If a porter finds a burlap bag containing about 15 pounds of fresh fish, he should 17.____
    A. sell it
    B. destroy it
    C. keep it
    D. turn it in

18. A porter must get a receipt for a lost article to prove that he 18.____
    A. found it
    B. received it
    C. turned it in
    D. knows what it is

19. A special messenger is NOT required to be used for a 19.____
    A. bag of 10 dollar bills
    B. silver-handled pistol
    C. gold candlestick
    D. genuine pearl necklace

20. A porter finding a box of flowers with a tag showing the addressee should 20.____
    A. deliver it
    B. turn it in
    C. telephone addressee
    D. take it to the Lost Property Office

Questions 21-25.

DIRECTIONS: Questions 21 through 25 are to be answered SOLELY on the basis of the following passage on BUS RADIO TRANSMISSION CODE.

BUS RADIO TRANSMISSION CODE

Buses are equipped with a 2-way radio system to aid the bus operator in the performance of his job. It is used primarily to transmit information to the Radio Dispatcher located in the Central Radio Operations Center. To assist the bus operator in the transmission of information without loss of time or possible confusion, the following Code is used:

Code Red Tag: To be used only in extreme emergency, such as police assistance in the event of a hold-up, assault, serious vandalism, etc. The bus operator transmitting a Red Tag Alert shall have priority over all other incoming calls. All other bus operators shall stand by until Dispatcher gives order to resume normal operations.
Code 1: Collision involving a bus.
Code 2: Passenger injured on board bus.
Code 3: Disabled bus.
Code 4: Bus blocked by fire apparatus, other vehicle, parade, etc.

21. If a bus operator observes a mugging taking place on his bus, he should radio a Code 21.____
   A. 1 B. 2 C. 3 D. 4

22. If a passenger trips and hurts himself on a bus, the bus operator should radio a Code 22.____
   A. 1 B. 2 C. 3 D. 4

23. If a bus is blocked by a street demonstration of marching adults, the bus operator should radio a Code 23.____
   A. 1 B. 2 C. 4 D. Red Tag

24. While a bus operator is reporting an injury to a passenger who fell and hurt his leg on the bus, a second bus operator interrupts this radio conversation with a Code Red Tag. 24.____
The FIRST bus operator should
   A. continue with his message so that the passenger may be aided quickly
   B. repeat his message since the interruption may have scrambled his voice
   C. immediately stop talking
   D. ask the second bus operator to wait until he has completed his message

25. If a bus engine stalls and cannot be restarted, the bus operator should radio a Code 25.____
   A. 1 B. 2 C. 3 D. Red Tag

KEY (CORRECT ANSWERS)

1.	C	11.	B
2.	C	12.	D
3.	B	13.	D
4.	C	14.	D
5.	D	15.	B
6.	D	16.	D
7.	D	17.	D
8.	D	18.	C
9.	D	19.	B
10.	A	20.	B

21.	D
22.	B
23.	C
24.	C
25.	C

CODING

EXAMINATION SECTION

COMMENTARY

An ingenious question-type called coding, involving elements of alphabetizing, filing, name and number comparison, and evaluative judgment and application, has currently won wide acceptance in testing circles for measuring clerical aptitude and general ability, particularly on the senior (middle) grades (levels).

While the directions for this question usually vary in detail, the candidate is generally asked to consider groups of names, codes, and numbers, and then, according to a given plan, to arrange codes in alphabetic order; to arrange these in numerical sequence; to re-arrange columns of names and numbers in correct order; to espy errors in coding; to choose the correct coding arrangement in consonance with the given directions and examples, etc.

This question-type appear to have few parameters in respect to form, substance, or degree of difficulty.

Accordingly, acquaintance with, and practice in, the coding question is recommended for the serious candidate.

TEST 1

DIRECTIONS: Questions 1 through 8 are to be answered on the basis of the code table and the instructions given below.

Code Letter for Traffic Problem	B	H	Q	J	F	L	M	I
Code Number for Action Taken	1	2	3	4	5	6	7	8

Assume that each of the capital letters on the above chart is a radio code for a particular traffic problem and that the number immediately below each capital letter is the radio code for the correct action to be taken to deal with the problem. For instance, "1" is the action to be taken to deal with problem "B", "2" is the action to be taken to deal with problem "H", and so forth.

In each question, a series of code letters is given in Column 1. Column 2 gives four different arrangements of code numbers. You are to pick the answer (A, B, C, or D) in Column 2 that gives the code numbers that match the code letters in the same order.

SAMPLE QUESTION

Column 1	Column 2
BHLFMQ	A. 125678
	B. 216573
	C. 127653
	D. 126573

According to the chart, the code numbers that correspond to these code letters are as follows: B – 1, M – 2, L – 6, F – 5, M – 7, Q – 3. Therefore, the right answer is 126573. This answer is D in Column 2.

Column 1	Column 2	
1. BHQLMI	A. 123456 B. 123567 C. 123678 D. 125678	1.____
2. HBJQLF	A. 214365 B. 213456 C. 213465 D. 214387	2.____
3. QHMLFJ	A. 321654 B. 345678 C. 327645 D. 327654	3.____
4. FLQJIM	A. 543287 B. 563487 C. 564378 D. 654378	4.____
5. FBIHMJ	A. 518274 B. 152874 C. 528164 D. 517842	5.____
6. MIHFQB	A. 872341 B. 782531 C. 782341 D. 783214	6.____
7. JLFHQIM	A. 465237 B. 456387 C. 4652387 D. 4562387	7.____
8. LBJQIFH	A. 614382 B. 6134852 C. 61437852 D. 61431852	8.____

KEY (CORRECT ANSWERS)

1.	C	5.	A
2.	A	6.	B
3.	D	7.	C
4.	B	8.	A

TEST 2

DIRECTIONS: Each question or incomplete statement is followed by several suggested answers or completions. Select the one that BEST answers the question or completes the statement. *PRINT THE LETTER OF THE CORRECT ANSWER IN THE SPACE AT THE RIGHT.*

Questions 1-5.

DIRECTIONS: Questions 1 through 5 are based on the following list showing the name and number of each of nine inmates.

1. Johnson	4. Thompson	7. Gordon
2. Smith	5. Frank	8. Porter
3. Edwards	6. Murray	9. Lopez

Each question consists of 3 sets of numbers and letters. Each set should consist of the numbers of three inmates and the first letter of each of their names. The letters should be in the same order as the numbers. In at least two of the three choices, there will be an error. On your answer sheet, mark only that choice in which the letters correspond with the numbers and are in the same order. If all three sets are wrong, mark choice D in your answer space.

SAMPLE QUESTION
A. 386 EPM
B. 542 FST
C. 474 LGT

Since 3 corresponds to E for Edwards, 8 corresponds to P for Porter, and 6 corresponds to M for Murray, choice A is correct and should be entered in your answer space. Choice B is wrong because letters T and S have been reversed. Choice C is wrong because the first number, which is 4, does NOT correspond with the first letter of choice C, which is L. It should have been T. If choice A were also wrong, then D would be the correct answer.

1. A. 382 EGS B. 461 TMJ C. 875 PLF 1.____

2. A. 549 FLT B. 692 MJS C. 758 GSP 2.____

3. A. 936 LEM B. 253 FSE C. 147 JTL 3.____

4. A. 569 PML B. 716 GJP C. 842 PTS 4.____

5. A. 356 FEM B. 198 JPL C. 637 MEG 5.____

Questions 6-10.

DIRECTIONS: Questions 6 through 10 are to be answered on the basis of the following information:

In order to make sure stock is properly located, incoming units are stored as follows:

STOCK NUMBERS	BIN NUMBERS
00100 – 39999	D30, L44
40000 – 69999	14L, D38
70000 – 99999	41L, 80D
100000 and over	614, 83D

Using the above table, choose the answer A, B, C, or D, which lists the correct Bin Number for the Stock Number given.

6. 17243 6.____
   A. 41L B. 83D C. 14L D. D30

7. 9219 7.____
   A. D38 B. L44 C. 614 D. 41L

8. 90125 8.____
   A. 41L B. 614 C. D38 D. D30

9. 10001 9.____
   A. L44 B. D38 C. 80D D. 83D

10. 200100 10.____
    A. 41L B. 14L C. 83D D. D30

KEY (CORRECT ANSWERS)

1.	B	6.	D
2.	D	7.	B
3.	A	8.	A
4.	C	9.	A
5.	C	10.	C

TEST 3

DIRECTIONS: Each question or incomplete statement is followed by several suggested answers or completions. Select the one that BEST answers the question or completes the statement. *PRINT THE LETTER OF THE CORRECT ANSWER IN THE SPACE AT THE RIGHT.*

Questions 1-9.

DIRECTIONS: Assume that the Police Department is planning to conduct a statistical study of individuals who have been convicted of crimes during a certain year. For the purpose of this study, identification numbers are being assigned to individuals in the following manner:

The first two digits indicate the age of the individual.
The third digit indicates the sex of the individual:
1. Male
2. Female

The fourth digit indicates the type of crime involved:
1. criminal homicide
2. forcible rape
3. robbery
4. aggravated assault
5. burglary
6. larceny
7. auto theft
8. other

The fifth and sixth digits indicate the month in which the conviction occurred:
01. January
02. February, etc.

Questions 1 through 9 are to be answered SOLELY on the basis of the above information and the following list of individuals and identification numbers.

Abbott, Richard	271304	Morris, Chris	212705
Collins, Terry	352111	Owens, William	231412
Elders, Edward	191207	Parker, Leonard	291807
George, Linda	182809	Robinson, Charles	311102
Hill, Leslie	251702	Sands, Jean	202610
Jones, Jackie	301106	Smith, Michael	42108
Lewis, Edith	402406	Turner, Donald	191601
Mack, Helen	332509	White, Barbara	242803

1. The number of women on the above list is 1.____
   A. 6 B. 7 C. 8 D. 9

2. The two convictions which occurred during February were for the crimes of 2.____
   A. aggravated assault and auto theft
   B. auto theft and criminal homicide
   C. burglary and larceny
   D. forcible rape and robbery

3. The ONLY man convicted of auto theft was 3.____
   A. Richard Abbott B. Leslie Hill
   C. Chris Morris D. Leonard Parker

4. The number of people on the list who were 25 years old or older is 4.____
   A. 6 B. 7 C. 8 D. 9

5. The OLDEST person on the list is 5.____
   A. Terry Collins B. Edith Lewis
   C. Helen Mack D. Michael Smith

6. The two people on the list who are the same age are 6.____
   A. Richard Abbott and Michael Smith
   B. Edward Elders and Donald Turner
   C. Linda George and Helen Mack
   D. Leslie Hill and Charles Robinson

7. A 28-year-old man who was convicted of aggravated assault in October would have identification number 7.____
   A. 281410 B. 281509 C. 282311 D. 282409

8. A 33-year-old woman convicted in April of criminal homicide would have identification number 8.____
   A. 331140 B. 331204 C. 332014 D. 332104

9. The number of people on the above list who were convicted during the first six months of the year is 9.____
   A. 6 B. 7 C. 8 D. 9

Questions 10-19.

DIRECTIONS: The following is a list of patients who were referred by various clinics to the laboratory for tests. After each name is a patient identification number. Questions 10 through 19 are to be answered on the basis of the information contained in this list and the explanation accompanying it.

The first digit refers to the clinic which made the referral:

1. cardiac
2. Renal
3. Pediatrics
4. Ophthalmology
5. Orthopedics
6. Hematology
7. Gynecology
8. Neurology
9. Gastroenterology

The second digit refers to the sex of the patient:
1. male
2. female

The third and fourth digits give the age of the patient
The last two digits give the day of the month the laboratory tests were performed

LABORATORY REFERRALS DURING JANUARY

Adams, Jacqueline	320917	Miller, Michael	511806
Black, Leslie	813406	Pratt, William	214411
Cook, Marie	511616	Rogers, Ellen	722428
Fisher, Pat	914625	Saunders, Sally	310229
Jackson, Lee	923212	Wilson, Jan	416715
James, Linda	624621	Wyatt, Mark	321326
Lane, Arthur	115702		

10. According to the list, the number of women referred to the laboratory during January was 10.____
A. 4 B. 5 C. 6 D. 7

11. The clinic from which the MOST patients were referred was 11.____
A. Cardiac
B. Gynecology
C. Ophthalmology
D. Pediatrics

12. The YOUNGEST patient referred from any clinic other than Pediatrics was 12.____
A. Leslie Black
B. Marie Cook
C. Arthur Lane
D. Sally Saunders

13. The number of patients whose laboratory tests were performed on or before January 16 was 13.____
A. 7 B. 8 C. 9 D. 10

14. The number of patients referred for laboratory tests who are under age 45 is 14.____
A. 7 B. 8 C. 9 D. 10

15. The OLDEST patient referred to the clinic during January was 15.____
A. Jacqueline Adams
B. Linda James
C. Arthur Lane
D. Jan Wilson

16. The ONLY patient treated in the Orthopedics clinic was 16.____
A. Marie Cook
B. Pat Fisher
C. Ellen Rogers
D. Jan Wilson

17. A woman, age 37 was referred from the Hematology clinic to the laboratory. Her laboratory tests were performed on January 9. Her identification number would be 17.____
A. 610937 B. 623709 C. 613790 D. 623790

18. A man was referred for lab tests from the Orthopedics clinic. He is 30 years old and his tests were performed on January 6. 18.____
His identification number would be
A. 413006 B. 510360 C. 513006 D. 513060

19. A 4-year-old boy was referred from the Pediatrics clinic to have laboratory tests on January 23. 19.____
His identification number was
A. 310422 B. 310423 C. 310433 D. 320403

KEY (CORRECT ANSWERS)

1.	B	11.	D
2.	B	12.	B
3.	B	13.	A
4.	D	14.	C
5.	D	15.	D
6.	B	16.	A
7.	A	17.	B
8.	D	18.	C
9.	C	19.	B
10.	B		

TEST 4

DIRECTIONS: Each question or incomplete statement is followed by several suggested answers or completions. Select the one that BEST answers the question or completes the statement. *PRINT THE LETTER OF THE CORRECT ANSWER IN THE SPACE AT THE RIGHT.*

Questions 1-10.

DIRECTIONS: Questions 1 through 10 are to be answered on the basis of the information and directions given below.

Assume that you are a Senior Stenographer assigned to the personnel bureau of a city agency. Your supervisor has asked you to classify the employees in your agency into the following five groups:

A. Employees who are college graduates, who are at least 35 years of age but less than 50, and who have been employed by the City for five years or more;
B. Employees who have been employed by the City for less than five years, who are not college graduates, and who earn at least $32,500 a year but less than $34,500;
C. Employees who have been City employees for five years or more, who are at least 21 years of age but less than 35, and who are not college graduates;
D. Employee who earn at least $34,500 a year but less than $36,000 who are college graduates, and who have been employed by the City for less than five years;
E. Employees who are not included in any of the foregoing groups.

NOTE: In classifying these employees you are to compute age and period of service as of <u>January 1, 2003</u>. In all cases, it is to be assumed that each employee has been employed continuously in City service. <u>In each question, consider only the information which will assist you in classifying each employee Any information which is of no assistance in classifying an employee would not be considered.</u>

SAMPLE: Mr. Brown, a 29-year-old veteran, was appointed to his present position of Clerk on June 1, 2000. He has completed two years of college. His present salary is $33,050.

The correct answer to this sample is B, since the employee has been employed by the City for less than five years, is not a college graduate, and earn at least $32,500 a year but less than $34,500.

Questions 1 through 10 contain excerpts from the personnel records of 10 employees in the agency. In the correspondingly numbered space at the right print the capital letter preceding the appropriate group into which you would place each employee.

1. Mr. James has been employed by the City since 1993, when he was graduated from a local college. Now 35 years of age, he earns $36,000 a year. 1.____

2. Mr. Worth began working in City service early in 1999. He was awarded his college degree in 1994, at the age of 21. As a result of a recent promotion, he now earns $34,500 a year. 2.____

3. Miss Thomas has been a City employee since August 1, 1998. Her salary is $34,500 a year. Miss Thomas, who is 25 years old, has had only three years of high school training. 3.____

4. Mr. Williams has had three promotions since entering City service on January 1, 1991. He was graduated from college with honors in 1974, when he was 20 years of age. His present salary is $37,000 a year. 4.____

5. Miss Jones left college after two years of study to take an appointment to a position in the City service paying $33,300 a year. She began work on March 1, 1997 when she was 19 years of age. 5.____

6. Mr. Smith was graduated from an engineering college with honors in January 1998 and became a City employee three months later. His present salary is $35,810. Mr. Smith was born in 1976. 6.____

7. Miss Earnest was born on May 31, 1979. Her education consisted of four years of high school and one year of business school. She was appointed as a typist in a City agency on June 1, 1997. Her annual salary is $33,500. 7.____

8. Mr. Adams, a 24-year-old clerk, began his City service on July 1, 1999, soon after being discharged from the U.S. Army. A college graduate, his present annual salary is $33,200. 8.____

9. Miss Charles attends college in the evenings, hoping to obtain her degree is 2004, when she will be 30 years of age. She has been a City employee since April 1998, and earns $33,350. 9.____

10. Mr. Dolan was just promoted to his present position after six years of City service. He was graduated from high school in 1982, when he was 18 years of age, but did not go on to college. Mr. Dolan's present salary is $33,500. 10.____

KEY (CORRECT ANSWERS)

1.	A	6.	D
2.	D	7.	C
3.	E	8.	E
4.	A	9.	B
5.	C	10.	E

TEST 5

DIRECTIONS: Questions 1 through 4 each contain five numbers that should be arranged in numerical order. The number with the lowest numerical value should be first and the number with the highest numerical value should be last. Pick that option which indicates the CORRECT order of the numbers.

Examples: A. 9; 18; 14; 15; 27
B. 9; 14; 15; 18; 27
C. 14; 15; 18; 27; 9
D. 9; 14; 15; 27; 18

The correct answer is B, which contains the proper arrangement of the five numbers.

1. A. 20573; 20753; 20738; 20837; 20098 1.____
B. 20098; 20753; 20573; 20738; 20837
C. 20098; 20573; 20753; 20837; 20738
D. 20098; 20573; 20738; 20753; 20837

2. A. 113492; 113429; 111314; 113114; 131413 2.____
B. 111314; 113114; 113429; 113492; 131413
C. 111314; 113429; 113492; 113114; 131413
D. 111314; 113114; 131413; 113429; 113492

3. A. 1029763; 1030421; 1035681; 1036928; 1067391 3.____
B. 1030421; 1029763; 1035681; 1067391; 1036928
C. 1030421; 1035681; 1036928; 1067391; 1029763
D. 1029763; 1039421; 1035681; 1067391; 1036928

4. A. 1112315; 1112326; 1112337; 1112349; 1112306 4.____
B. 1112306; 1112315; 1112337; 1112326; 1112349
C. 1112306; 1112315; 1112326; 1112337; 1112349
D. 1112306; 1112326; 1112315; 1112337; 1112349

KEY (CORRECT ANSWERS)

1. D
2. B
3. A
4. C

TEST 6

DIRECTIONS: The phonetic filing system is a method of filing names in which the alphabet is reduced to key code letters. The six key letters and their equivalents are as follows:

KEY LETTERS	EQUIVALENTS
b	p, f, v
c	s, k, g, j, q, x, z
d	t
l	none
m	n
r	none

A key letter represents itself.
Vowels (a, e, i, o, and u) and the letters w, h, and y are omitted.
For example, the name GILMAN would be represented as follows:

G is represented by the key letter C.
I is a vowel and is omitted.
L is a letter and represents itself.
M is a key letter and represents itself.
A is a vowel and is omitted.
N is represented by the key letter M.

Therefore, the phonetic filing code for the name GILMAN is CLMM.

Answer Questions 1 through 10 based on the information below.

1. The phonetic filing code for the name FITZGERALD would be 1.____
   A. BDCCRLD B. BDCRLD C. BDZCRLD D. BTZCRLD

2. The phonetic filing code CLBR may represent any one of the following names EXCEPT 2.____
   A. Calprey B. Flower C. Glover D. Silver

3. The phonetic filing code LDM may represent any one of the following names EXCEPT 3.____
   A. Halden B. Hilton C. Walton D. Wilson

4. The phonetic filing code for the name RODRIGUEZ would be 4.____
   A. RDRC B. RDRCC C. RDRCZ D. RTRCC

5. The phonetic filing code for the name MAXWELL would be 5.____
   A. MCLL B. MCWL C. MCWLL D. MXLL

6. The phonetic filing code for the name ANDERSON would be 6.____
   A. AMDRCM B. ENDRSM C. MDRCM D. NDERCN

7. The phonetic filing code for the name SAVITSKY would be 7.____
   A. CBDCC B. CBDCY C. SBDCC D. SVDCC

8. The phonetic filing code CMC may represent any one of the following names EXCEPT 8.____
   A. James B. Jayes C. Johns D. Jones

9. The ONLY one of the following names that could be represented by the phonetic filing code CDDDM would be 9.____
   A. Catalano B. Chesterton C. Cittadino D. Cuttlerman

10. The ONLY one of the following names that could be represented by the phonetic filing code LLMCM would be 10.____
    A. Ellington B. Hallerman C. Inslerman D. Willingham

KEY (CORRECT ANSWERS)

1.	A	6.	C
2.	B	7.	A
3.	D	8.	B
4.	B	9.	C
5.	A	10.	D

NAME AND NUMBER CHECKING

EXAMINATION SECTION

TEST 1

DIRECTIONS: Questions 1 through 17 consist of sets of names and addresses. In each question, the name and address in Column II should be an exact copy of the name and address in Column I.
If there is:
a mistake only in the name, mark your answer A;
a mistake only in the address, mark your answer B;
a mistake in both name and address, mark your answer C;
No mistake in either name or address, mark your answer D.

<u>Sample Question</u>

Column I	Column II
Christina Magnusson 288 Greene Street New York, N.Y. 10003	Christina Magnusson 288 Greene Street New York, N.Y. 10013

Since there is a mistake only in the address (the zip code should be 10003 instead of 10013), the answer to the sample question is B.

	COLUMN I	COLUMN II	
1.	Ms. Joan Kelly 313 Franklin Avenue Brooklyn, N.Y. 11202	Ms. Joan Kielly 318 Franklin Ave. Brooklyn, N.Y. 11202	1.____
2.	Mrs. Eileen Engel 47-24 86 Road Queens, N.Y. 11122	Mrs. Ellen Engel 47-24 86 Road Queens, New York 11122	2.____
3.	Marcia Michaels 213 E. 81 St. New York, N.Y. 10012	Marcia Michaels 213 E. 81 St. New York, N.Y. 10012	3.____
4.	Rev. Edward J. Smyth 1401 Brandeis Street San Francisco, Calif. 96201	Rev. Edward J. Smyth 1401 Brandies Street San Francisco, Calif. 96201	4.____
5.	Alicia Rodriguez 24-68 82 St. Elmhurst, N.Y. 11122	Alicia Rodriguez 2468 81 St. Elmhurst, N.Y. 11122	5.____

	COLUMN I	COLUMN II	
6.	Ernest Eisemann 21 Columbia St. New York, N.Y. 10007	Ernest Eisermann 21 Columbia St. New York, N.Y. 10007	6.____
7.	Mr. & Mrs. George Petersson 87-11 91st Avenue Woodhaven, N.Y. 11421	Mr. & Mrs. George Peterson 87-11 91st Avenue Woodhaven, N.Y. 11421	7.____
8.	Mr. Ivan Klebnikov 1848 Newkirk Avenue Brooklyn, N.Y. 11226	Mr. Ivan Klebikov 1848 Newkirk Avenue Brooklyn, N.Y. 11622	8.____
9.	Mr. Samuel Rothfleisch 71 Pine Street New York, N.Y. 10005	Samuel Rothfleisch 71 Pine Street New York, N.Y. 100005	9.____
10.	Mrs. Isabel Tonnessen 198 East 185th Street Bronx, N.Y. 10458	Mrs. Isabel Tonnessen 189 East 185th Street Bronx, N.Y. 10348	10.____
11.	Esteban Perez 173 Eighth Street Staten Island, N.Y. 10306	Estaban Perez 173 Eighth Street Staten Island, N.Y. 10306	11.____
12.	Esta Wong 141 West 68 St. New York, N.Y. 10023	Esta Wang 141 West 68 St. New York, N.Y. 10023	12.____
13.	Dr. Alberto Grosso 3475 12th Avenue Brooklyn, N.Y. 11218	Dr. Alberto Grosso 3475 12th Avenue Brooklyn, N.Y. 11218	13.____
14.	Mrs. Ruth Bortias 482 Theresa Ct. Far Rockaway, N.Y. 11691	Ms. Ruth Bortlas 482 Theresa Ct. Far Rockaway, N.Y. 11169	14.____
15.	Mr. & Mrs. Howard Fox 2301 Sedgwick Ave. Bronx, N.Y. 10468	Mr. & Mrs. Howard Fox 231 Sedgwick Ave. Bronx, N.Y. 10468	15.____
16.	Miss Marjorie Black 223 East 23 Street New York, N.Y. 10010	Miss Margorie Black 223 East 23 Street New York, N.Y. 10010	16.____

	COLUMN I	COLUMN II	
17.	Michelle Herman 806 Valley Rd. Old Tappan, N.J. 07675	Michelle Hermann 806 Valley Dr. Old Tappan, N.J. 07675	17.____

KEY (CORRECT ANSWERS)

1.	C	7.	A	13.	D
2.	A	8.	C	14.	C
3.	D	9.	D	15.	B
4.	B	10.	B	16.	A
5.	B	11.	A	17.	C
6.	A	12.	D		

TEST 2

DIRECTIONS: Questions 1 through 15 are to be answered SOLELY on the instructions given below. *PRINT THE LETTER OF THE CORRECT ANSWER IN THE SPACE AT THE RIGHT.*

INSTRUCTIONS

In each of the following questions, the 3-line name and address in Column I is the master-list entry, and the 3-line entry in Column II is the information to be checked against the master list. If there is one line that does not match, mark your answer A; if there are two lines that do not match, mark your answer B; if all three lines do not match, mark your answer C; if the lines all match exactly, mark your answer D.

Sample Question

Column I	Column II
Mark L. Field	Mark L. Field
11-09 Price Park Blvd.	11-99 Prince Park Way
Bronx, N.Y. 11402	Bronx, N.Y. 11401

The first lines in each column match exactly. The second lines do not match since 11-09 does not match 11-99; and Blvd. does not match Way. The third lines do not match either since 11402 does not match 11401. Therefore, there are two lines that do not match, and the CORRECT answer is B.

	COLUMN I	COLUMN II	
1.	Jerome A. Jackson 1243 14th Avenue New York, N.Y. 10023	Jerome A. Johnson 1234 14th Avenue New York, N.Y. 10023	1.____
2.	Sophie Strachtheim 33-28 Connecticut Ave. Far Rockaway, N.Y. 11697	Sophie Strachtheim 33-28 Connecticut Ave. Far Rockaway, N.Y. 11697	2.____
3.	Elisabeth N.T. Gorrell 256 Exchange St. New York, N.Y. 10013	Elizabeth N.T. Gorrell 256 Exchange St. New York, N.Y. 10013	3.____
4.	Maria J. Gonzalez 7516 E. Sheepshead Rd. Brooklyn, N.Y. 11240	Maria J. Gonzalez 7516 N. Shepshead Rd. Brooklyn, N.Y. 11240	4.____
5.	Leslie B. Brautenweiler 21 57A Seiler Terr. Flushing, N.Y. 11367	Leslie B. Brautenwieler 21-75A Seiler Terr. Flushing, N.J. 11367	5.____

	COLUMN I	COLUMN II	
6.	Rigoberto J. Peredes 157 Twin Towers, #18F Tottenville, S. I., N.Y,	Rigoberto J. Peredes 157 Twin Towers, #18F Tottenville, S.I., N.Y.	6.____
7.	Pietro F. Albino P.O. Box 7548 Floral Park, N.Y. 11005	Pietro F. Albina P.O. Box 7458 Floral Park, N.Y. 11005	7.____
8.	Joanne Zimmerman Bldg. SW, Room 314 532-4601	Joanne Zimmermann Bldg. SW, Room 314 532-4601	8.____
9.	Carlyle Whetstone Payroll Div. –A, Room 212A 262-5000, ext. 471	Carlyle Whetstone Payroll Div. –A, Room 212A 262-5000, ext. 417	9.____
10.	Kenneth Chiang Legal Council, Room 9745 (201) 416-9100, ext. 17	Kenneth Chiang Legal Counsel, Room 9745 (201) 416-9100, Ext. 17	10.____
11.	Ethel Koenig Personnel Services Division, Room 433; 635-7572	Ethel Hoenig Personal Services Division, Room 433; 635-7527	11.____
12.	Joyce Ehrhardt Office of the Administrator, Room W56; 387-8706	Joyce Ehrhart Office of the Administrator, Room W56; 387-7806	12.____
13.	Ruth Lang EAM Bldg., Room C101 625-2000, ext. 765	Ruth Lang EAM Bldg., Room C110 625-2000, ext. 765	13.____
14.	Anne Marie Ionozzi Investigations, Room 827 576-4000, ext. 832	Anna Marie Ionozzi Investigation, Room 827 566-4000, ext. 832	14.____
15.	Willard Jameson Fm C Bldg., Room 687 454-3010	Willard Jamieson Fm C Bldg., Room 687 454-3010	15.____

KEY (CORRECT ANSWERS)

1.	B	6.	D	C	C
2.	D	7.	B	12.	B
3.	A	8.	D	13.	A
4.	A	9.	B	14.	C
5.	C	10.	A	15.	A

TEST 3

DIRECTIONS: Questions 1 through 10 are to be answered on the basis of the following instructions. *PRINT THE LETTER OF THE CORRECT ANSWER IN THE SPACE AT THE RIGHT.*

<u>INSTRUCTIONS</u>

For each such set of names, addresses, and numbers listed in Columns I and II, select your answer from the following options:

The names in Columns I and II are different,
The addresses in Columns I and II are different,
The numbers in Columns I and II are different,
The names, addresses, and numbers in Columns I and II are identical.

	COLUMN I	COLUMN II	
1.	Francis Jones 62 Stately Avenue 96-12446	Francis Jones 62 Stately Avenue 96-21446	1.____
2.	Julio Montez 19 Ponderosa Road 56-73161	Julio Montez 19 Ponderosa Road 56-71361	2.____
3.	Mary Mitchell 2314 Melbourne Drive 68-92172	Mary Mitchell 2314 Melbourne Drive 68-92172	3.____
4.	Harry Patterson 25 Dunne Street 14-33430	Harry Patterson 25 Dunne Street 14-34330	4.____
5.	Patrick Murphy 171 West Hosmer Street 93-81214	Patrick Murphy 171 West Hosmer Street 93-18214	5.____
6.	August Schultz 816 St. Clair Avenue 53-40149	August Schultz 816 St. Claire Avenue 53-40149	6.____
7.	George Taft 72 Runnymede Street 47-04033	George Taft 72 Runnymede Street 47-04023	7.____
8.	Angus Henderson 1418 Madison Street 81-76375	Angus Henderson 1318 Madison Street 81-76375	8.____

	COLUMN I	COLUMN II	
9.	Carolyn Mazur 12 Riverview Road 38-99615	Carolyn Mazur 12 Rivervane Road 38-99615	9.____
10.	Adele Russell 1725 Lansing Lane 72-91962	Adela Russell 1725 Lansing Lane 72-91962	10.____

KEY (CORRECT ANSWERS)

1.	C	6.	B
2.	C	7.	C
3.	D	8.	D
4.	C	9.	B
5.	C	10.	A

TEST 4

DIRECTIONS: Questions 1 through 20 test how good you are at catching mistakes in typing or printing. In each question, the name and address in Column II should be an exact copy of the name and address in Column I. Mark your answer
A. If there is no mistake in either name or address;
B. If there is a mistake in both name and address;
C. If there is a mistake only in the name;
D. If there is a mistake only in the address.
PRINT THE LETTER OF THE CORRECT ANSWER IN THE SPACE AT THE RIGHT.

	COLUMN I	COLUMN II	
1.	Milos Yanocek 33-60 14 Street Long Island City, N.Y. 11011	Milos Yanocek 33-60 14 Street Long Island City, N.Y. 11001	1.____
2.	Alphonse Sabattelo 24 Minnetta Lane New York, N.Y. 10006	Alphonse Sabbattelo 24 Minetta Lane New York, N.Y. 10006	2.____
3.	Helen Steam 5 Metropolitan Oval Bronx, N.Y. 10462	Helene Stearn 5 Metropolitan Oval Bronx, N.Y. 10462	3.____
4.	Jacob Weisman 231 Francis Lewis Boulevard Forest Hills, N.Y. 11325	Jacob Weisman 231 Francis Lewis Boulevard Forest Hills, N.Y. 11325	4.____
5.	Riccardo Fuente 134 West 83 Street New York, N.Y. 10024	Riccardo Fuentes 134 West 88 Street New York, N.Y. 10024	5.____
6.	Dennis Lauber 52 Avenue D Brooklyn, N.Y. 11216	Dennis Lauder 52 Avenue D Brooklyn, N.Y. 11216	6.____
7.	Paul Cutter 195 Galloway Avenue Staten Island, N.Y. 10356	Paul Cutter 175 Galloway Avenue Staten Island, N.Y. 10365	7.____
8.	Sean Donnelly 45-58 41 Avenue Woodside, N.Y. 11168	Sean Donnelly 45-58 41 Avenue Woodside, N.Y. 11168	8.____
9.	Clyde Willot 1483 Rockaway Avenue Brooklyn, N.Y. 11238	Clyde Willat 1483 Rockaway Avenue Brooklyn, N.Y. 11238	9.____

	COLUMN I	COLUMN II	
10.	Michael Stanakis 419 Sheriden Avenue Staten Island, N.Y. 10363	Michael Stanakis 419 Sheraden Avenue Staten Island, N.Y. 10363	10.____
11.	Joseph DiSilva 63-84 Saunders Road Rego Park, N.Y. 11431	Joseph Disilva 64-83 Saunders Road Rego Park, N.Y. 11431	11.____
12.	Linda Polansky 2224 Fendon Avenue Bronx, N.Y. 20464	Linda Polansky 2255 Fenton Avenue Bronx, N.Y. 10464	12.____
13.	Alfred Klein 260 Hillside Terrace Staten Island, N.Y. 15545	Alfred Klein 260 Hillside Terrace Staten Island, N.Y. 15545	13.____
14.	William McDonnell 504 E. 55 Street New York, N.Y. 10103	William McConnell 504 E. 55 Street New York, N.Y. 10108	14.____
15.	Angela Cipolla 41-11 Parson Avenue Flushing, N.Y. 11446	Angela Cipola 41-11 Parsons Avenue Flushing, N.Y. 11446	15.____
16.	Julie Sheridan 1212 Ocean Avenue Brooklyn, N.Y. 11237	Julia Sheridan 1212 Ocean Avenue Brooklyn, N.Y. 11237	16.____
17.	Arturo Rodriguez 2156 Cruger Avenue Bronx, N.Y. 10446	Arturo Rodrigues 2156 Cruger Avenue Bronx, N.Y. 10446	17.____
18.	Helen McCabe 2044 East 19 Street Brooklyn, N.Y. 11204	Helen McCabe 2040 East 19 Street Brooklyn, N.Y. 11204	18.____
19.	Charles Martin 526 West 160 Street New York, N.Y. 10022	Charles Martin 526 West 160 Street New York, N.Y. 10022	19.____
20.	Morris Rabinowitz 31 Avenue M Brooklyn, N.Y. 11216	Morris Rabinowitz 31 Avenue N Brooklyn, N.Y. 11216	20.____

KEY (CORRECT ANSWERS)

1.	D	11.	B
2.	B	12.	D
3.	C	13.	A
4.	A	14.	B
5.	B	15.	B
6.	C	16.	C
7.	D	17.	C
8.	A	18.	D
9.	B	19.	A
10.	D	20.	D

TEST 5

DIRECTIONS: In copying the addresses below from Column A to the same line in Column B, an Agent-in-Training made some errors. For Questions 1 through 5, if you find that the agent made an error in
only one line, mark your answer A;
only two lines, mark your answer B;
only three lines, mark your answer C;
all four lines, mark your answer D.

EXAMPLE

COLUMN A	COLUMN B
24 Third Avenue	24 Third Avenue
5 Lincoln Road	5 Lincoln Street
50 Central Park West	6 Central Park West
37-21 Queens Boulevard	21-37 Queens Boulevard

Since errors were made on only three lines, namely the second, third, and fourth, the CORRECT answer is C.

PRINT THE LETTER OF THE CORRECT ANSWER IN THE SPACE AT THE RIGHT.

	COLUMN A	COLUMN B	
1.	57-22 Springfield Boulevard	75-22 Springfield Boulevard	1.____
	94 Gun Hill Road	94 Gun Hill Avenue	
	8 New Dorp Lane	8 New Drop Lane	
	36 Bedford Avenue	36 Bedford Avenue	
2.	538 Castle Hill Avenue	538 Castle Hill Avenue	2.____
	54-15 Beach Channel Drive	54-15 Beach Channel Drive	
	21 Ralph Avenue	21 Ralph Avenue	
	162 Madison Avenue	162 Morrison Avenue	
3.	49 Thomas Street	49 Thomas Street	3.____
	27-21 Northern Blvd.	21-27 Northern Blvd.	
	86 125th Street	86 125th Street	
	872 Atlantic Ave.	872 Baltic Ave,	
4.	261-17 Horace Harding Expwy.	261-17 Horace Harding Pkwy.	4.____
	191 Fordham Road	191 Fordham Road	
	6 Victory Blvd.	6 Victoria Blvd.	
	552 Oceanic Ave.	552 Ocean Ave.	
5.	90-05 38th Avenue	90-05 36th Avenue	5.____
	19 Central Park West	19 Central Park East	
	9281 Avenue X	9281 Avenue X	
	22 West Farms Square	22 West Farms Square	

KEY (CORRECT ANSWERS)

1. C
2. A
3. B
4. C
5. B

TEST 6

DIRECTIONS: For Questions 1 through 10, choose the letter in Column II next to the number which EXACTLY matches the number in Column I. *PRINT THE LETTER OF THE CORRECT ANSWER IN THE SPACE AT THE RIGHT.*

	COLUMN I	COLUMN II	
1.	14235	A. 13254 B. 12435 C. 13245 D. 14235	1.____
2.	70698	A. 90768 B. 60978 C. 70698] D. 70968	2.____
3.	11698	A. 11689 B. 11986 C. 11968 D. 11698	3.____
4.	50497	A. 50947 B. 50497 C. 50749 D. 54097	4.____
5.	69635	A. 60653 B. 69630 C. 69365 D. 69635	5.____
6.	1201022011	A. 1201022011 B. 1201020211 C. 1202012011 D. 1021202011	6.____
7.	3893981389	A. 3893891389 B. 3983981389 C. 3983891389 D. 3893981389	7.____
8.	4765476589	A. 4765476598 B. 4765476588 C. 4765476589 D. 4765746589	8.____

9. 8679678938

A. 8679687938
B. 8679678938
C. 8697678938
D. 8678678938

9.____

10. 6834836932

A. 6834386932
B. 6834836923
C. 6843836932
D. 6834836932

10.____

Questions 11-15.

DIRECTIONS: For Questions 11 through 15, determine how many of the symbols in Column Z are exactly the same as the symbol in Column Y.
If none is exactly the same, answer A;
If only one symbol is exactly the same, answer B;
If two symbols are exactly the same, answer C;
If three symbols are exactly the same, answer D.

	COLUMN Y	COLUMN Z	
11.	A123B1266	A123B1366 A123B1266 A133B1366 A123B1266	11.____
12.	CC28D3377	CD22D3377 CC38D3377 CC28C3377 CC28D2277	12.____
13.	M21AB201X	M12AB201X M21AB201X M21AB201Y M21BA201X	13.____
14.	PA383Y744	AP383Y744 PA338Y744 PA388Y744 PA383Y774	14.____
15.	PB2Y8893	PB2Y8893 PB2Y8893 PB3Y8898 PB2Y8893	15.____

KEY (CORRECT ANSWERS)

1.	D	6.	A	11.	C
2.	C	7.	D	12.	A
3.	D	8.	C	13.	B
4.	B	9.	B	14.	A
5.	D	10.	D	15.	D

POLICE SCIENCE NOTES

POLICE COMMUNICATIONS

Communication can be defined as the transfer of information from one person to another. It can be accomplished in a variety of ways including the spoken word, written message, signal or electrical device. Geographically, communication involves the transmission of messages from one point to another, either interdepartmentally or intradepartmentally. Any exchange of words, messages, or signals in connection with police action may be classified as police communications.

History

Police communications, contrary to many modern beliefs, are as old as the police service itself. In 17th century England, policemen carried bells or lanterns for identification and as signal devices to give warnings or to summon assistance. The 18th century saw little improvement in police signaling equipment. Police officers in the 19th century utilized whistles, night sticks, and even their pistols as signal devices. The 20th century brought the introduction of electrical devices to the field of police communications. The horn, bell, light, telegraph, telephone, radio-telegraph, radio, radar, and now television, afford communications with infinitely increased efficiency. These developments also have produced great strides in the area of speed, range, and area coverage.

Along with these developments in the technical aspects of police communications, the written reporting system of law enforcement agencies have become considerably more sophisticated with the use of automatic and electronic data storage and processing equipment becoming more and more common. This progress has resulted in more accurate, complete, and easily recoverable information for police use.

The rapid growth of police communication probably is the best indication of its success in police administration. It has enabled a remarkable increase in the promptness and effectiveness of police action, especially in emergencies where time is of utmost importance, and closer and more effective control over patrolmen in the field. Most recently developed and available are: two-way radios small enough to be carried on an officer's belt; printout or screen display devices mounted in patrol cars with computer inquiry capability; and automatic query/response devices which show dispatchers or supervisors the geographic locations of patrol cars by radio direction finding systems. Advances in radio communication render perhaps the most important innovations in police methods since the introduction of fingerprinting.

Present Practice

Today's tools of communication are allowing police departments, both large and small, to increase the extent and efficiency of their service. Hardly a single police action is taken that does not involve some sort of communication. Original complaints are usually made to the police department by use of citizen-placed telephone calls. The information is relayed to police dispatchers or other appropriate personnel by use of interoffice phones or by use of mechanical devices, such as the pneumatic tube. In many cases two-way radio is used to relay information to patrol vehicles or to other police departments.

Also helping to stretch the police potential are systems of communication involving teletype, radiotelegraph, land-wire telegraph, long-distance phone circuits, interconnected computer and photo transmitting machines.

These are but a sample of what make up the network of communication found in most police departments. These tools plus proper techniques are invaluable in accomplishing the necessary steps to deal with natural disasters or nuclear attacks. Therefore, knowledge of such tools and techniques are imperative to successful actions of local police auxiliary units.

Telephone Procedures

The citizen's first contact with the police department is often a telephone conversation with an officer. On the telephone you are the police department's voice and whatever you say and how you say it creates for the citizen an impression of the department to that citizen. Every time you pick up the phone you are doing a public relations job. It may be good, bad, or indifferent. Why not always try for the good public relations job?

When considering proper procedures for the use of the telephone, courtesy and consideration are always the keywords. Even when receiving calls from persons who are agitated or excited the proper action remains much the same as in normal telephone calls. Since a large part of police telephone work is receiving calls the following procedures are essential ones.

1. Identify yourself immediately after answering.
2. Speak courteously.
3. Have pad and pencil handy-makes notes when necessary.

On the other hand, when *you* make a call follow the same basic guides of courtesy and consideration. This may be stated as follows:

1. Have in mind what you wish to know or say when your call is answered.
2. Identify yourself and state your business.
3. Have pad and pencil available-make notes when necessary.

Reaching for a telephone is one of our most frequent and familiar gestures. However, this does not guarantee good telephone usage. Proper procedures can result in good telephone usage and are important to proper police work.

Radio Procedure

Two-way radio might well be considered the backbone of police communications. In many instances the proper use of this instrument may well mean the difference between success or failure in any given situation. In general, the same guides apply as did to good telephone procedures, namely, courtesy and consideration. However, a few specific guides are identified for your use.

To transmit a message:

1. Be certain the dispatcher is not busy transmitting other messages.
2. Contact dispatcher, giving your identification, and then wait for dispatcher to answer.
3. Begin your message after the dispatcher has answered you.

While transmitting a message:

1. Speak distinctly into the microphone as in ordinary conversation. Too loud a voice distorts the reception.
2. Speak slowly.
3. Keep messages brief.
4. Mentally rehearse your message before transmitting.
5. Never use vulgar language.

The final rule cannot be overemphasized. Not only is such language in poor taste, but is prohibited by regulations of the FCC. Furthermore, any excess language used, and vulgar language is excess, may well confuse or distort the meaning of your message.

In learning to use radio communications effectively it is necessary to master the codes and specific procedures in effect in your local police department. Appendix II gives some samples of such procedures.

Emergency Information Media

In addition to the telephone and radio communications of the police service, during a CD emergency the auxiliary policeman will need to receive and act on messages disseminated by public information media (radio and television broadcasts, newspapers, etc.) as part of the emergency information program. Although these messages will be intended for the general public, they will also convey information of value to the auxiliary policeman in the performance of his duties. For example, in many local civil defense plans provision is made for certain radio stations to remain on the air as part of the Emergency Broadcasting System, and their broadcasts will convey official information on such matters as warning conditions and last-minute instructions regarding movement to shelters or relocation areas.

www.ingramcontent.com/pod-product-compliance
Lightning Source LLC
Chambersburg PA
CBHW082212300426
44117CB00016B/2774